ALTO CLARINET FINGERING CHARTS
Scales & Songs

Thank you	2
Let's Begin!	3
E♭ Alto Clarinet Finger Zones	4
Learning to Play Alto Clarinet	5
Scales for Alto Clarinet	6
C Major Scale (Up)	7
C Major Scale (Down)	8
G Major Scale (Low)	9
G Major Scale (Higher)	10
F Major Scale (Low)	11
F Major Scale (Higher)	12
D Major Scale Ascending	13
D Major Scale Descending	14
B♭ Major Scale (Low)	15
B♭ Major Scale (Higher)	16
A Major (Ascending)	17
A Major (Descending)	18
What is Your Embouchure?	19
Playing Tips	20
E Major Scale (Low)	21
E Major Scale (Higher)	22
E♭ Major Scale (Low)	23
E♭ Major Scale (Higher)	24
B Major Ascending	25
B Major Descending	26
A♭ Major Scale Ascending	27
A♭ Major Scale Descending	28
G♭ Major Scale (Low)	29
G♭ Major Scale (Higher)	30
D♭ Major Scale Ascending	31
D♭ Major Scale Descending	32
Chromatic Scale, E♭	33
Mary Had a Little Lamb	34
Twinkle Twinkle Little Star	36
Frère Jacques (Brother John)	38
It's a Jazzy Day!	40
Tips for Playing Alto Clarinet	42
Ring Around the Rosie	43
Pop Goes the Weasel	44
Camptown Races	46
Row Row Row Your Boat	48
Hot Cross Buns	50
London Bridge is Falling Down	52
That's What's the Matter	54
She'll Be Comin' 'Round the Mountain	56
Jingle Bells	58
This Old Man	60
E♭ Alto Clarinet Fingering Chart	61
E♭ Alto Clarinet History	64

Kimber Books

ISBN: 978-0-9988430-8-7
© 2025 The Martin Freres Company, Merimax, LLC
All Rights Reserved

Thank you!

Thank you for purchasing Alto Clarinet Fingering Charts, Scales & Songs. This book is E♭ Alto Clarinet music for absolute beginners.

As a beginner alto clarinetist, you've embarked on an adventure that is as rewarding as it is exciting. This book was designed with you in mind, to help you learn quickly and gain confidence by combining scales with songs that are fun and easy to play. With fingering charts displayed right below each note, you'll find it easier to focus on your playing without getting stuck on figuring out finger positions.

Each song has a QR Code to scan that brings you directly to the audio file for the music sheet. Listen before you play. Give it a try!

We truly hope this book helps you hit your first sweet notes and gives you the joy of performing music right away. Whether you're playing for yourself or sharing your new skills with others, remember to have fun and enjoy every step of your musical journey.

Happy playing!
Martin Freres

Let's Begin!

Learning to play the E♭ alto clarinet can feel tricky at first, especially when trying to figure out which fingers to use for the notes on the page. That's why this book has fingering charts right below each note. These charts make it much easier to focus on playing instead of guessing. Here's how to use them.

Understand the Fingering Chart
Each note comes with a fingering diagram that shows you exactly which keys to press and holes to cover.

- **Black circles** mean you should press those keys.
- **Open circles** mean those key cups stay untouched.
- **Black keys** mean you press those keys.

The fingering chart shown here is used for all the scales and songs in this book. On the music staff, the names of the notes are written above the staff to help you know what to play. Under each note, you'll see a fingering diagram that shows you where to put your fingers on the clarinet. This makes it easier to match the notes to the proper finger positions.

**Notes to Play:
Letter above - Note below**

E♭ Alto Clarinet Fingering

For each note, cover only the key cups or press the keys that are solid black.

By using the E♭ alto clarinet fingering charts, you'll learn faster and have more fun playing, now!

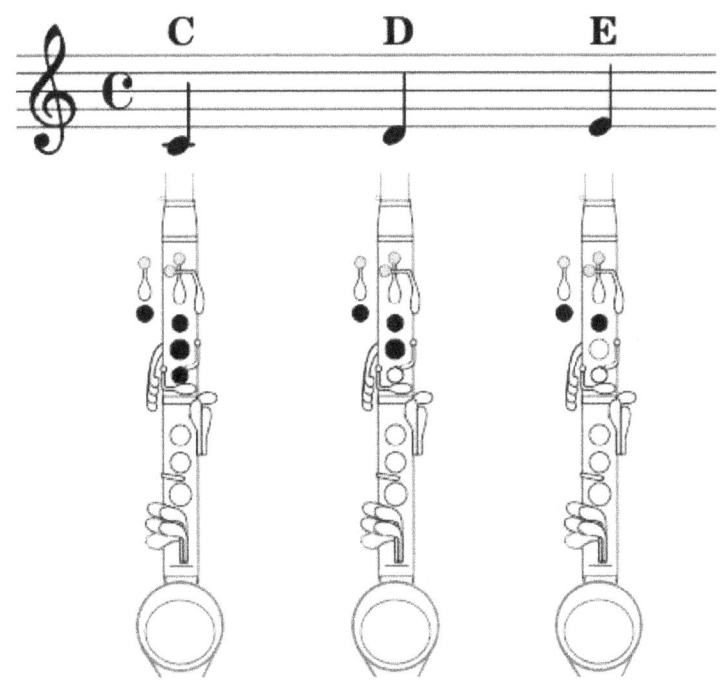

E♭ Alto Clarinet Finger Zones

Left Hand Finger Zones

The left hand finger zones on the clarinet are really important for playing a lot of the notes. Your left thumb rests on the thumb key cup on the back of the clarinet in the thumb zone, helping to support the instrument. Just above the thumb key cup is the register key, which you press with your thumb to play higher notes. On the front of the clarinet, your index finger covers the first key cup and can also press some nearby keys when needed. Your middle finger covers the second key cup, and your ring finger covers the third key cup. Your pinky controls the left-hand pinky zone keys, which are used for certain notes. Keep your fingers relaxed and close to their zones for smoother playing.

Right Hand Finger Zones

The right hand finger zones on the clarinet are just as important as the left for playing notes. Your thumb supports the clarinet from underneath, resting on the thumb rest to help balance the instrument. On the front, your index finger covers the fourth key cup and can press the trill keys when needed. Your middle finger covers the fifth key cup. In the ring finger zone there is a key and the sixth key cup. Below the sixth key cup are extra keys that your pinky finger controls in the pinky zone. These larger keys help you play lower notes, and your pinky will switch between them as needed. Keeping your fingers relaxed and in the right positions makes it easier to move smoothly between notes and play with better accuracy.

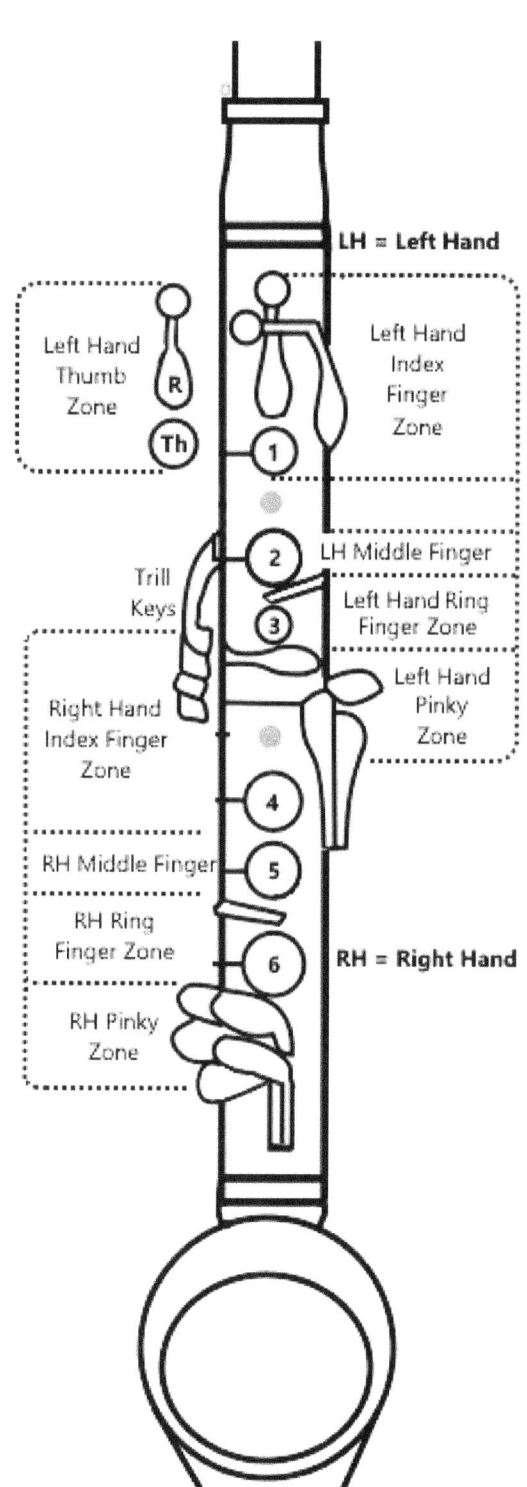

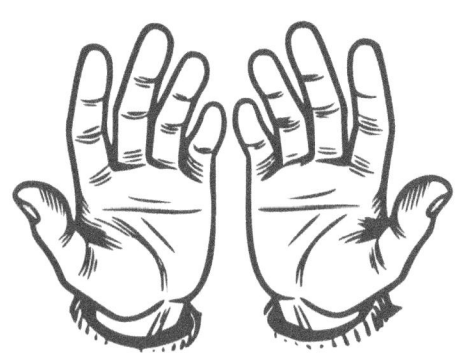

Which Finger Goes Where?

Learning to Play Alto Clarinet

Practice Scales First
The scales provided in this book are a great way to get used to the notes and their fingerings. Play through each scale slowly, making sure you match the note on the page with the correct fingering on your clarinet. Practice them until you can play smoothly without needing to check the fingering every time.

Use the Charts While Learning Songs
When you start playing songs, keep using the fingering charts as a guide. Play one note at a time and check your fingers if you need to. After a while, your fingers will begin to remember where to go, and you can follow the music sheet instead of the fingering charts.

Listen for Accuracy
Even if your fingers are in the right spots, your sound might still not be quite right if your breath control or mouth positioning (embouchure) isn't right. Use the charts to make sure your fingers are correct, but also focus on creating a clear, steady sound for each note.

Move Away from the Charts
As you get better, challenge yourself to play scales and songs by looking only at the notes on the staff. Let your fingers do the work from memory. The more you practice this way, the more confident and independent you'll become.

Use the Charts When You Need Help
If you're struggling with a note or forgetting a fingering, don't worry, just look at the fingering charts. They're there to help you when you need a quick reminder.

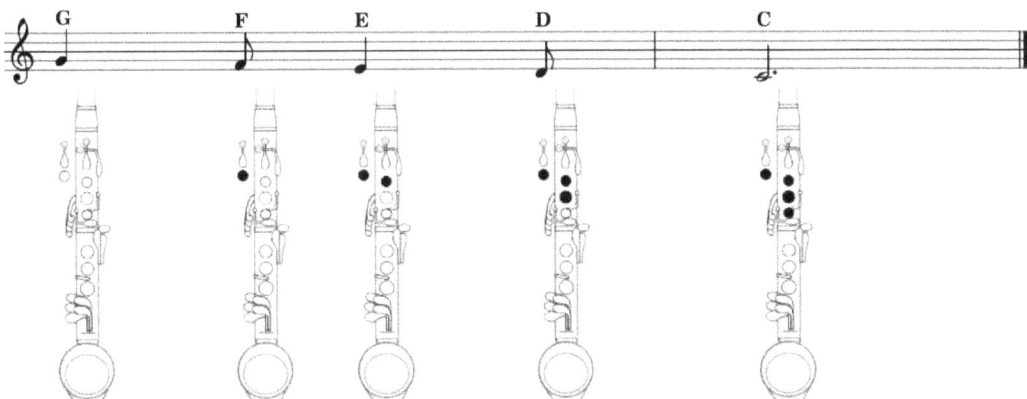

By practicing with these charts and gradually using them less, you'll build strong skills faster and with less frustration. Always remember, the goal is not just to play notes, it's to make music. With time and effort, you'll be playing with confidence and having fun. So, let's get started. You've got this!

Scales for Alto Clarinet

Major scales are like the building blocks of music. They're the foundation for nearly every song you hear, whether it's a pop tune, a movie soundtrack, or classical symphony. For E♭ alto clarinet players, mastering major scales helps you build strong fingers, improve your tone, and play with confidence. Since the clarinet is a E♭ instrument, the notes you read and play sound different from the ones on a piano. For example, when you play a C on the clarinet, it actually sounds like an E♭ on the piano. Pretty cool, right?

Why do we learn scales? Well, scales teach your fingers to move smoothly between notes, which is important for playing fast or tricky parts in songs. Scales also train your ears to recognize the sound of each key, making it easier to play melodies and harmonies in tune. Think of it like learning the alphabet before writing stories. It's hard to create music if you don't know the *language* of scales!

We'll start with the simplest scales and work our way up to the ones with more flats (♭) or sharps (#). In this book, we'll follow this order: C, G, F, D, B♭, A, E, E♭, B, A♭, G♭, and D♭. The C scale is a great place to begin because it has no sharps or flats, all notes in the scale are natural (♮) notes! As you progress, you'll tackle scales like B♭ and A♭, which include flats, and eventually get to G♭ and D♭, which are more challenging and sound amazing.

Here's a bit of history: scales have been around for centuries and were first written down by musicians in ancient Greece! The major scale we use today became popular in the 1600s and 1700s when composers like Bach and Mozart used it to write their music. When you practice your scales, you're following in the footsteps of musicians from hundreds of years ago. Plus, the better you know your scales, the more prepared you'll be to play solos, join bands, or even compose your own music.

Musical scales are like the steps of a ladder, helping you climb higher in your musical skills. Each rung shows how practicing scales builds your ability to play songs and understand music, one note at a time!

Let's start with the C Major Scale. The C major scale is often the first scale musicians learn because it's the simplest, it has no sharps or flats, just natural ♮ notes (C, D, E, F, G, A, B, and back to C). On the clarinet, this scale helps you get comfortable with finger patterns and smooth transitions between notes. It's like the starting line for your musical journey, giving you a solid foundation to build on. Plus, since so many pieces of music are written in C major, it's a great way to dive into playing real songs!

So, grab your alto clarinet and let's start PLAYING NOW!

C Major Scale (Up)

Practicing the C major scale trains your ear to recognize the sound of a major key, which is important for playing songs and understanding how music works. The C major scale includes the notes C, D, E, F, G, A, and B.

Remember, each note comes with a fingering diagram showing you which keys to press.

- Black circles mean you should press those keys.
- Open circles mean those key cups stay untouched.
- Black keys mean you press those keys.

Let's play the C major scale up, also known as **ascending** (low notes to high notes). Watch out for that big change!

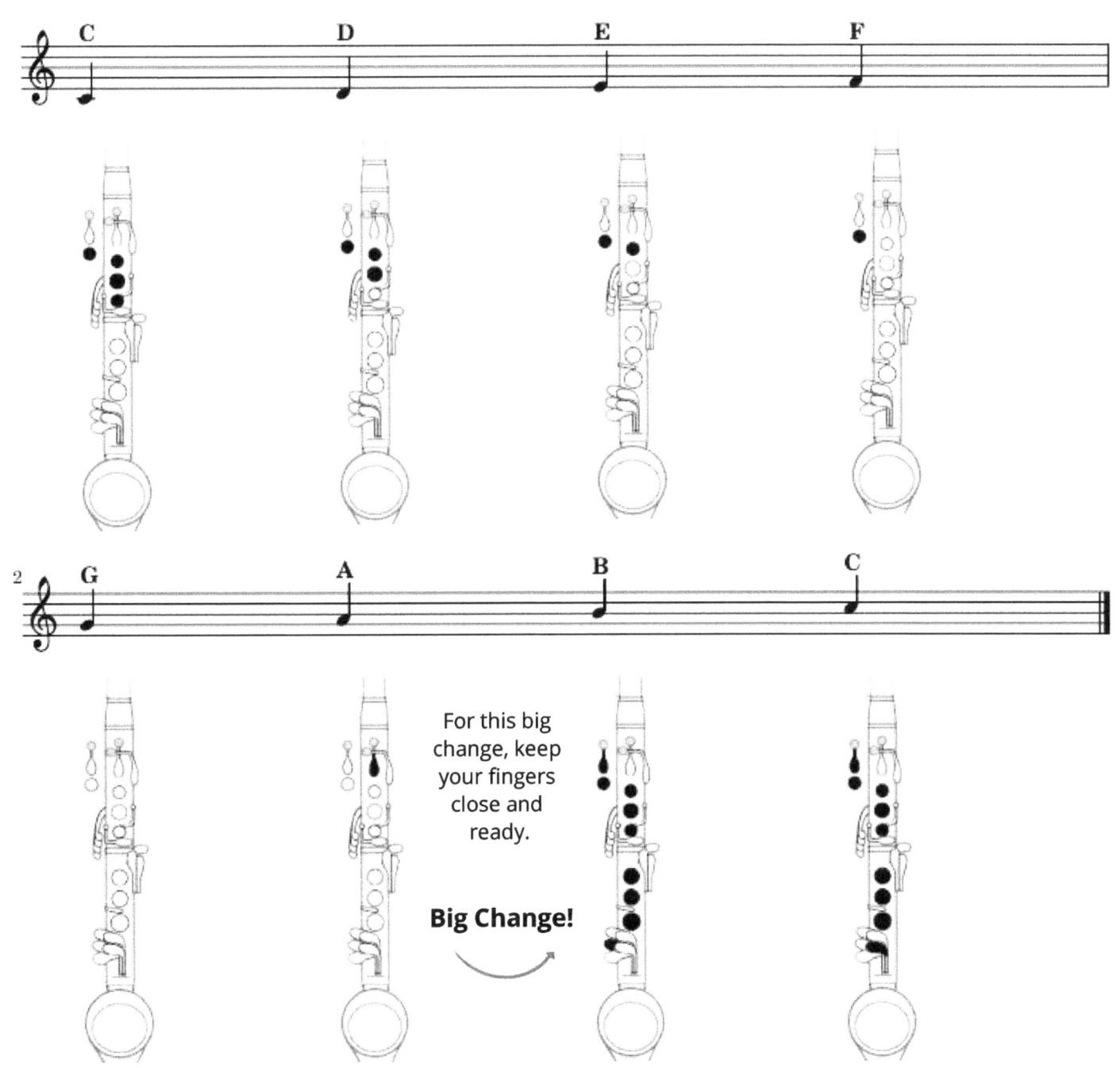

C Major Scale (Down)

Remember, each note comes with a fingering diagram showing you which keys to press.

- Black circles mean you should press those keys.
- Open circles mean those key cups stay untouched.
- Black keys mean you press those keys.

Let's play the C major scale down, which is also known as **descending** (high notes to low notes)!

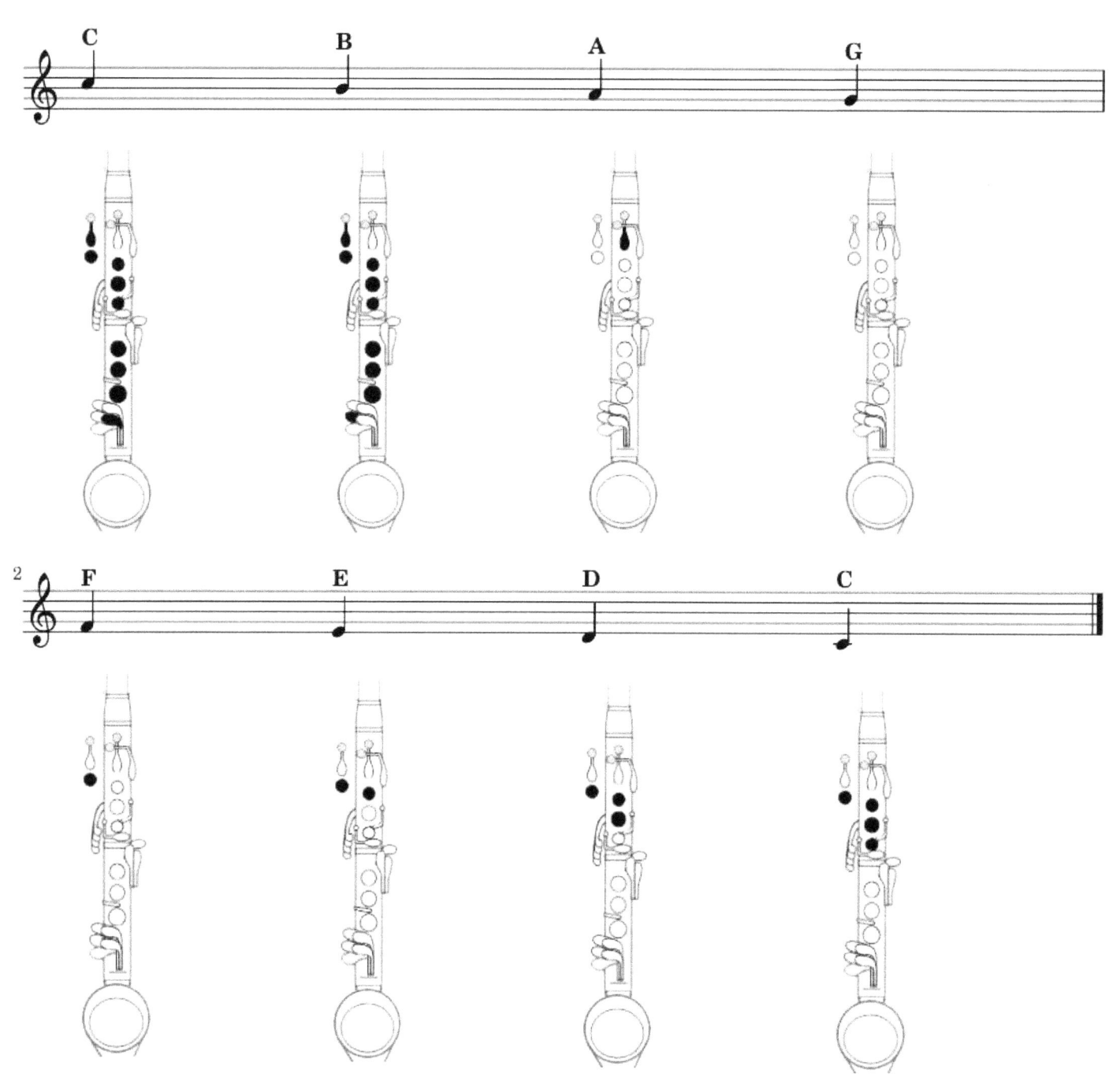

G Major Scale (Low)

OK, you're ready for the low G major scale. We call it "low" because the scale begins at the lowest possible G note for the G major scale on an E♭ alto clarinet. The G major scale includes the notes G, A, B, C, D, E, and F# (F sharp). Sharp means the note sounds slightly higher in tone.

Remember, each note comes with a fingering diagram showing you which keys to press.

- Black circles mean you should press those keys.
- Open circles mean those key cups stay untouched.
- Black keys mean you press those keys.

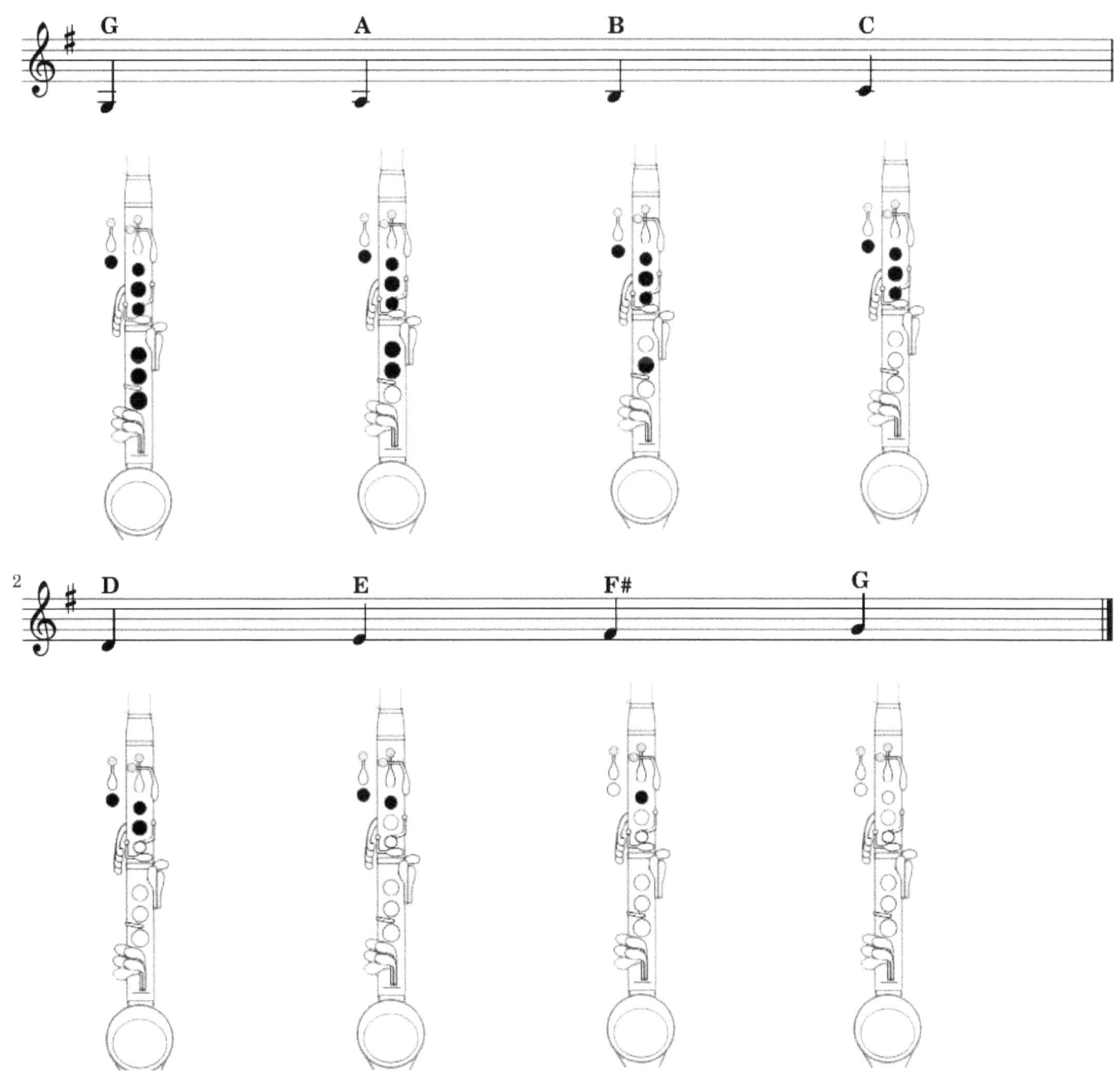

G Major Scale (Higher)

Let's try the G major scale one octave higher. Playing one octave higher means playing the same notes as we did before in G major (page 9), but at higher in pitch.

This one starts easy but watch out for that Big Change!

Remember, each note comes with a fingering diagram showing you which keys to press.

- Black circles mean you should press those keys.
- Open circles mean those key cups stay untouched.
- Black keys mean you press those keys.

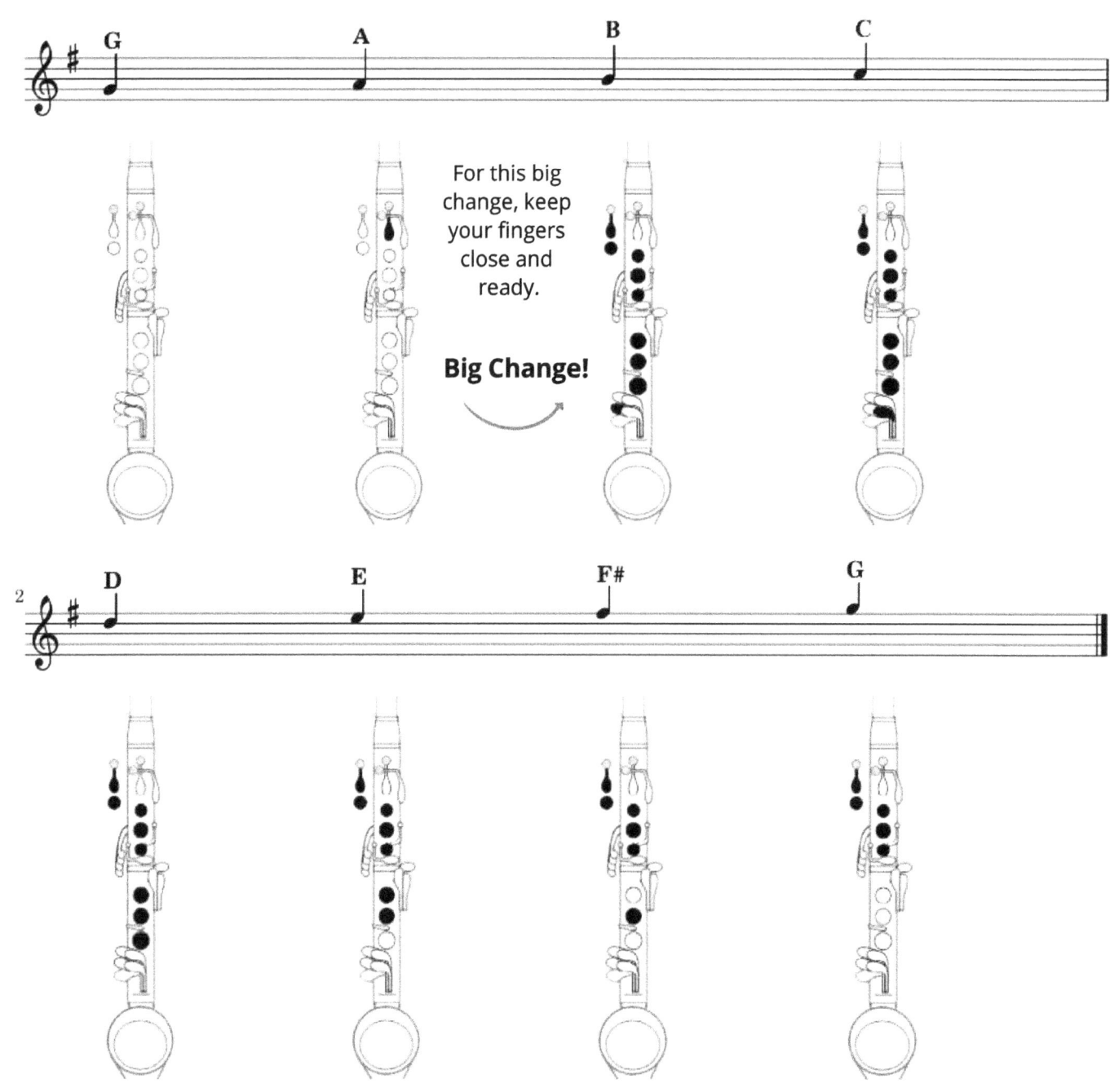

F Major Scale (Low)

Let's tackle the F major scale (low). This scale makes your fingers really work to start. But, for each note you play, you get to remove a finger! Take your time. Stop blowing, remove a finger, start blowing. That's it!

Remember, each note comes with a fingering diagram showing you which keys to press.

 - Black circles mean you should press those keys.
 - Open circles mean those key cups stay untouched.
 - Black keys mean you press those keys.

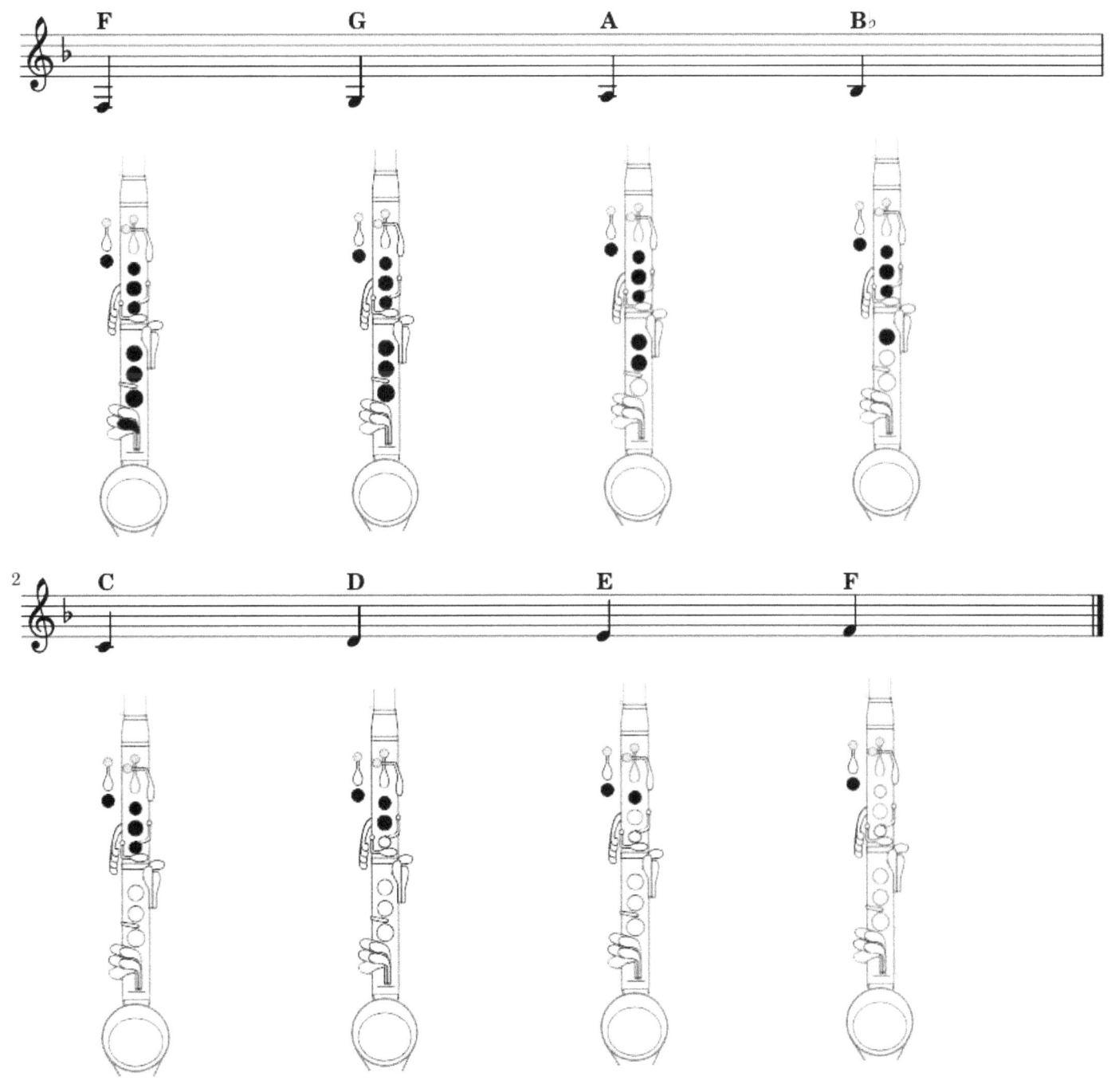

F Major Scale (Higher)

Let's tackle the F major scale in the higher octave. The jump from B♭ to C can be hard to do at first. Practice B♭ to C back to B♭ as many times as you need to until you can make a smooth sounding change between the notes.

Remember, each note comes with a fingering diagram showing you which keys to press.

- Black circles mean you should press those keys.
- Open circles mean those key cups stay untouched.
- Black keys mean you press those keys.

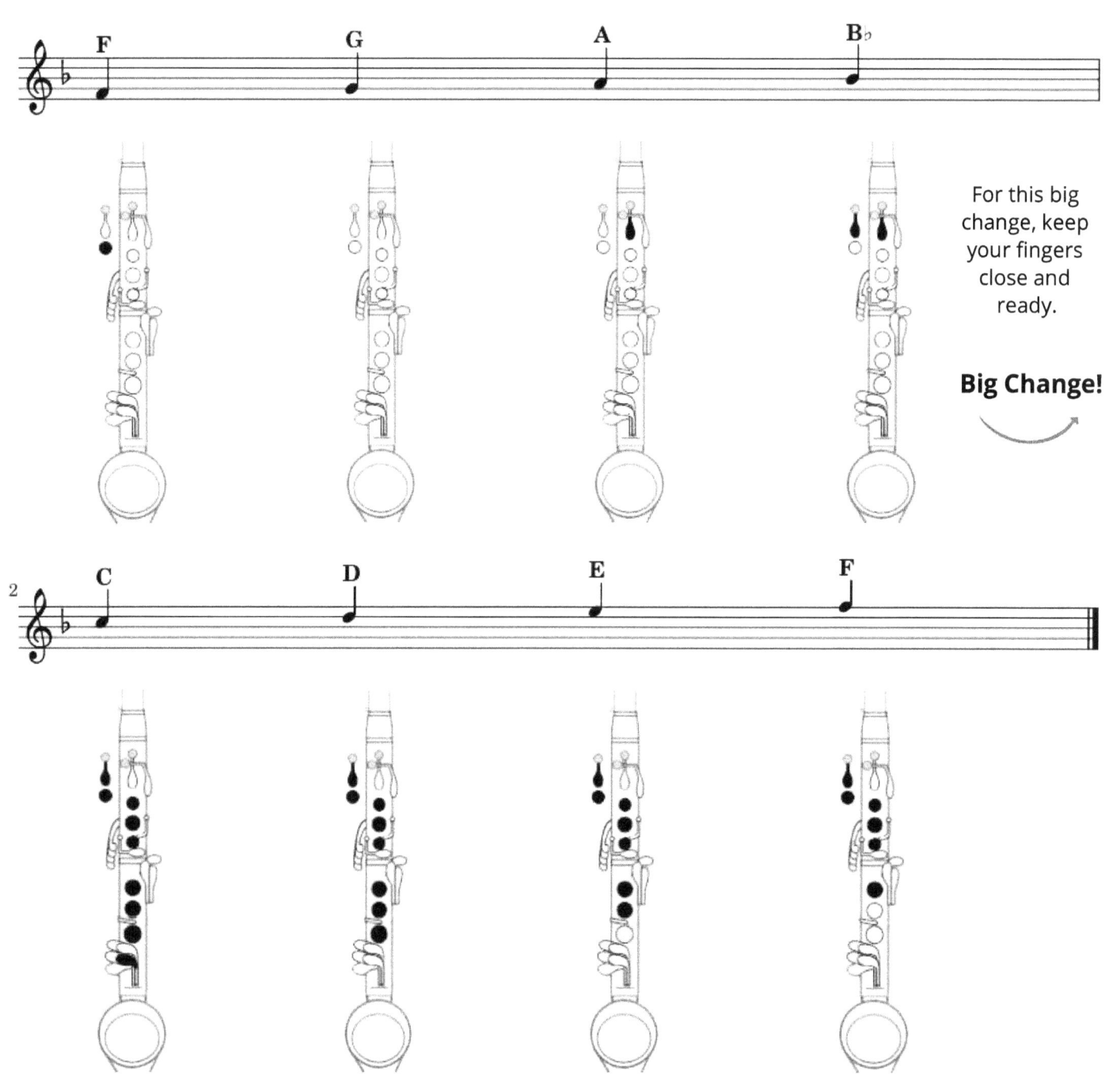

For this big change, keep your fingers close and ready.

Big Change!

D Major Scale Ascending

Let's work on the D major scale ascending. The D major scale includes the notes D, E, F#, G, A, B, and C#.

Remember, each note comes with a fingering diagram showing you which keys to press.

- Black circles mean you should press those keys.
- Open circles mean those key cups stay untouched.
- Black keys mean you press those keys.

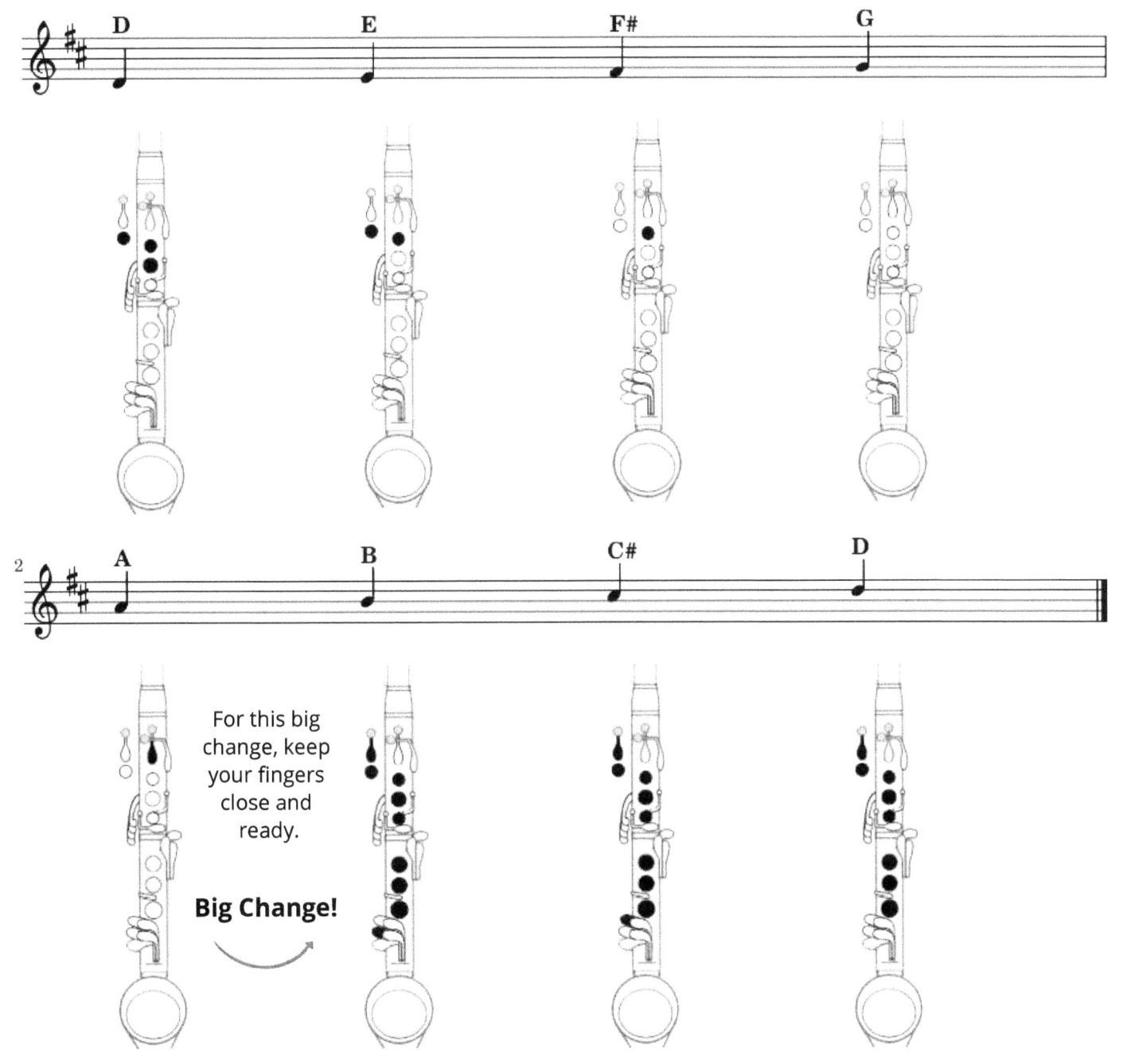

D Major Scale Descending

Now it's time for the D major scale descending.

Remember, each note comes with a fingering diagram showing you which keys to press.

- Black circles mean you should press those keys.
- Open circles mean those key cups stay untouched.
- Black keys mean you press those keys.

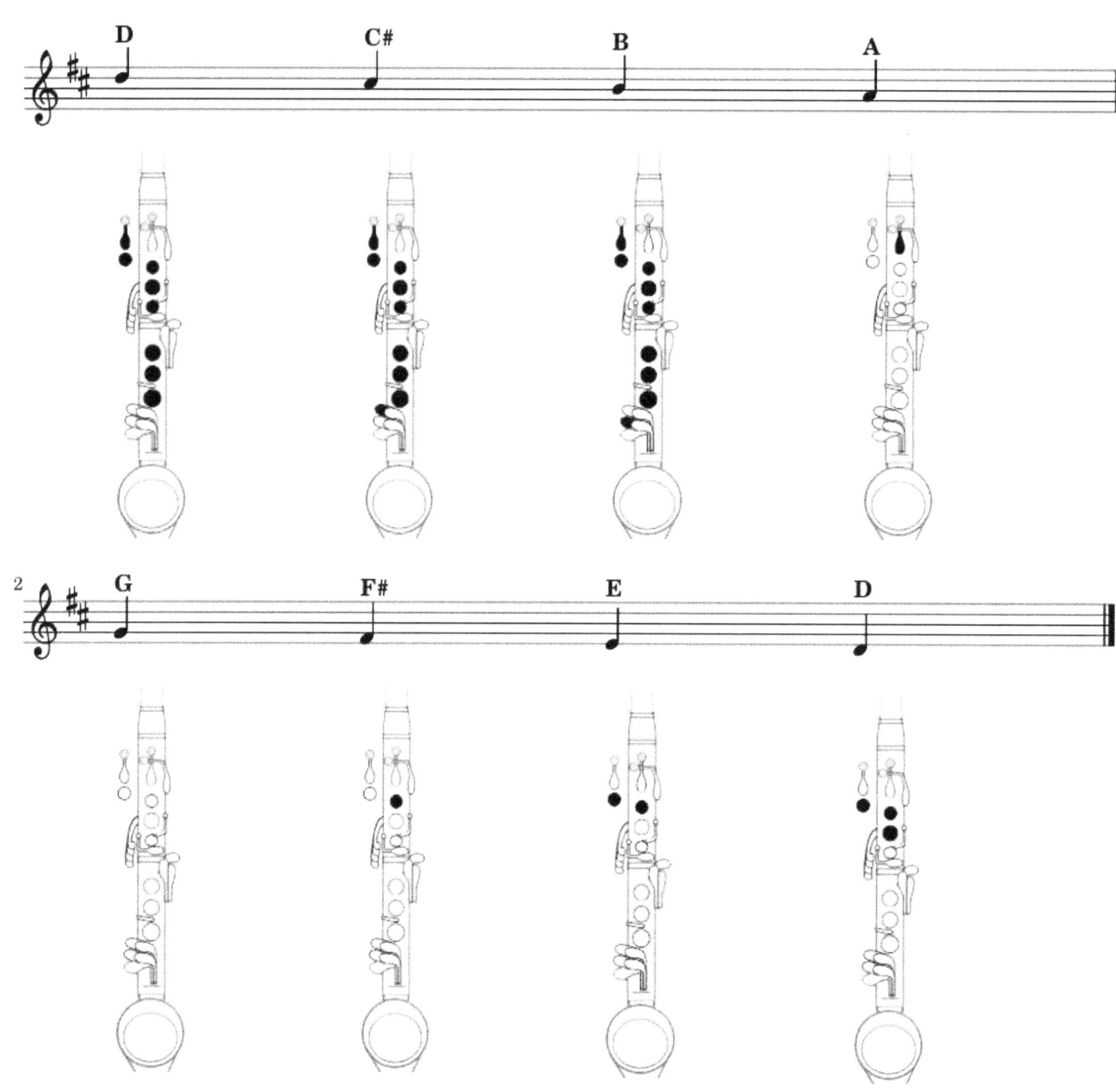

B♭ Major Scale (Low)

Let's work on the B♭ major scale (low). The B♭ major scale includes the notes B♭, C, D, E♭, F, G, and A.

Remember, each note comes with a fingering diagram showing you which keys to press.

- Black circles mean you should press those keys.
- Open circles mean those key cups stay untouched.
- Black keys mean you press those keys.

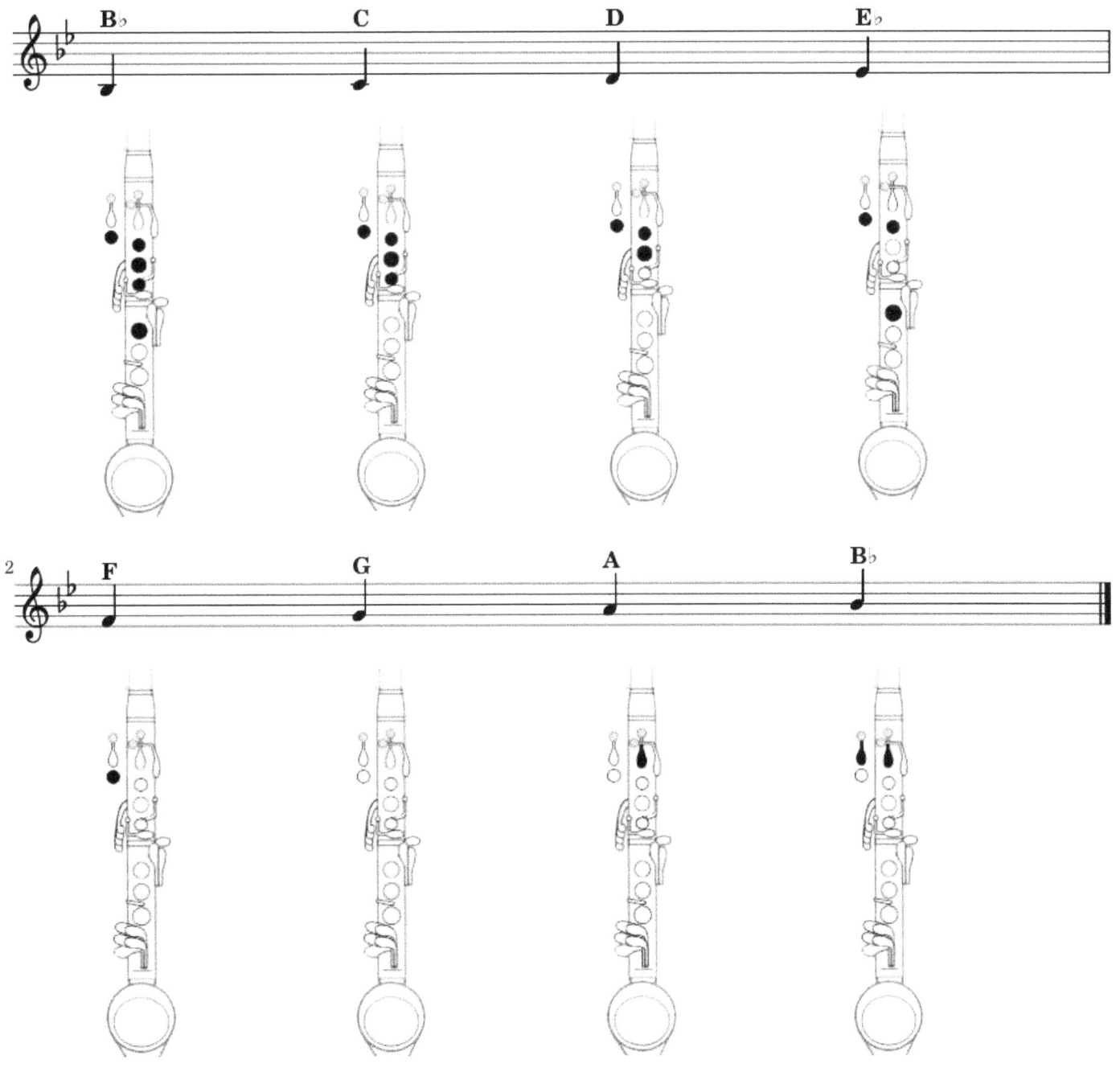

B♭ Major Scale (Higher)

Let's work on the B♭ major scale in the higher octave. You've got this!

Remember, each note comes with a fingering diagram showing you which keys to press.

- Black circles mean you should press those keys.
- Open circles mean those key cups stay untouched.
- Black keys mean you press those keys.

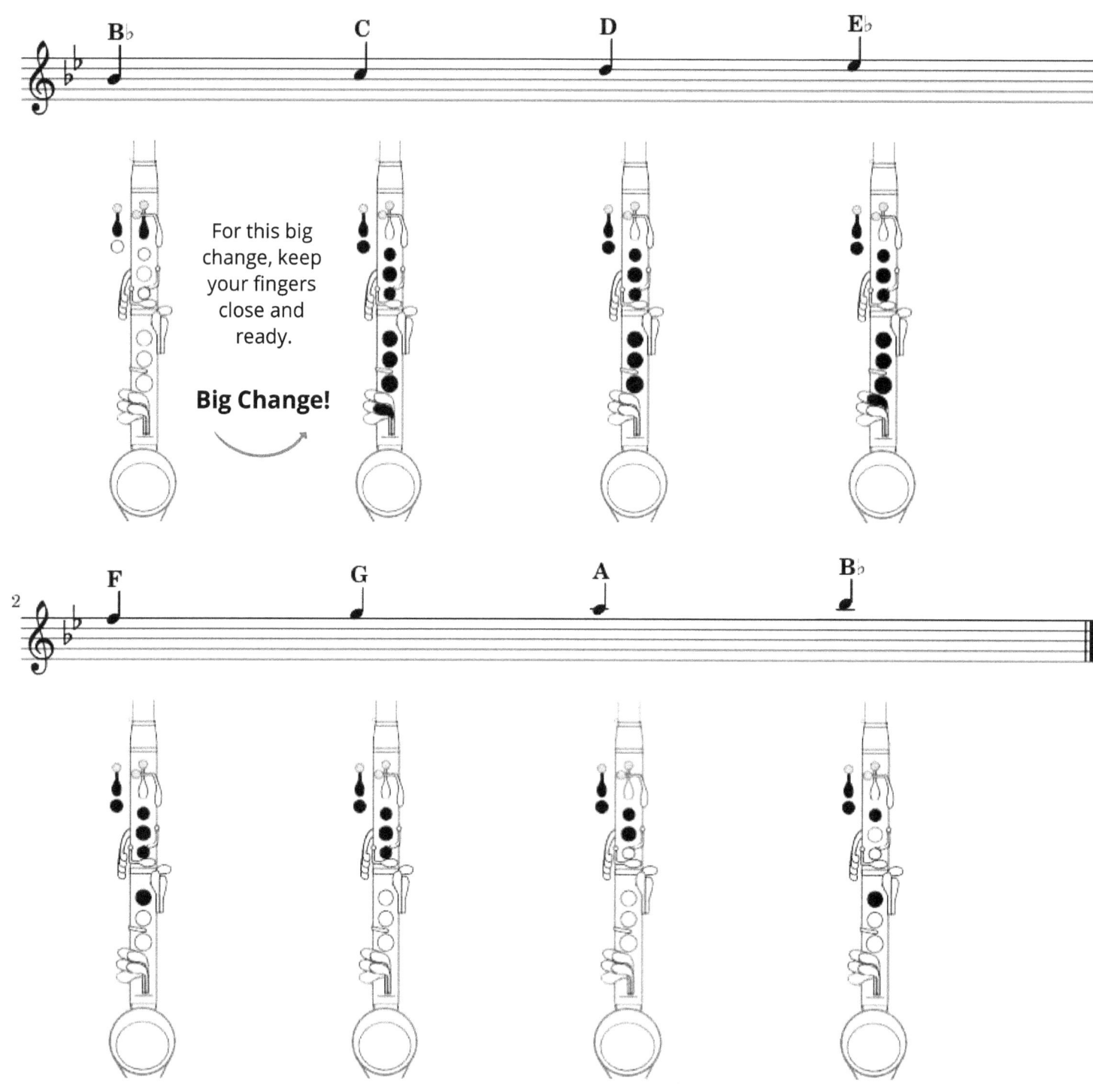

A Major Scale Ascending

How about the A major scale ascending? Give it a try!

Remember, each note comes with a fingering diagram showing you which keys to press.

- Black circles mean you should press those keys.
- Open circles mean those key cups stay untouched.
- Black keys mean you press those keys.

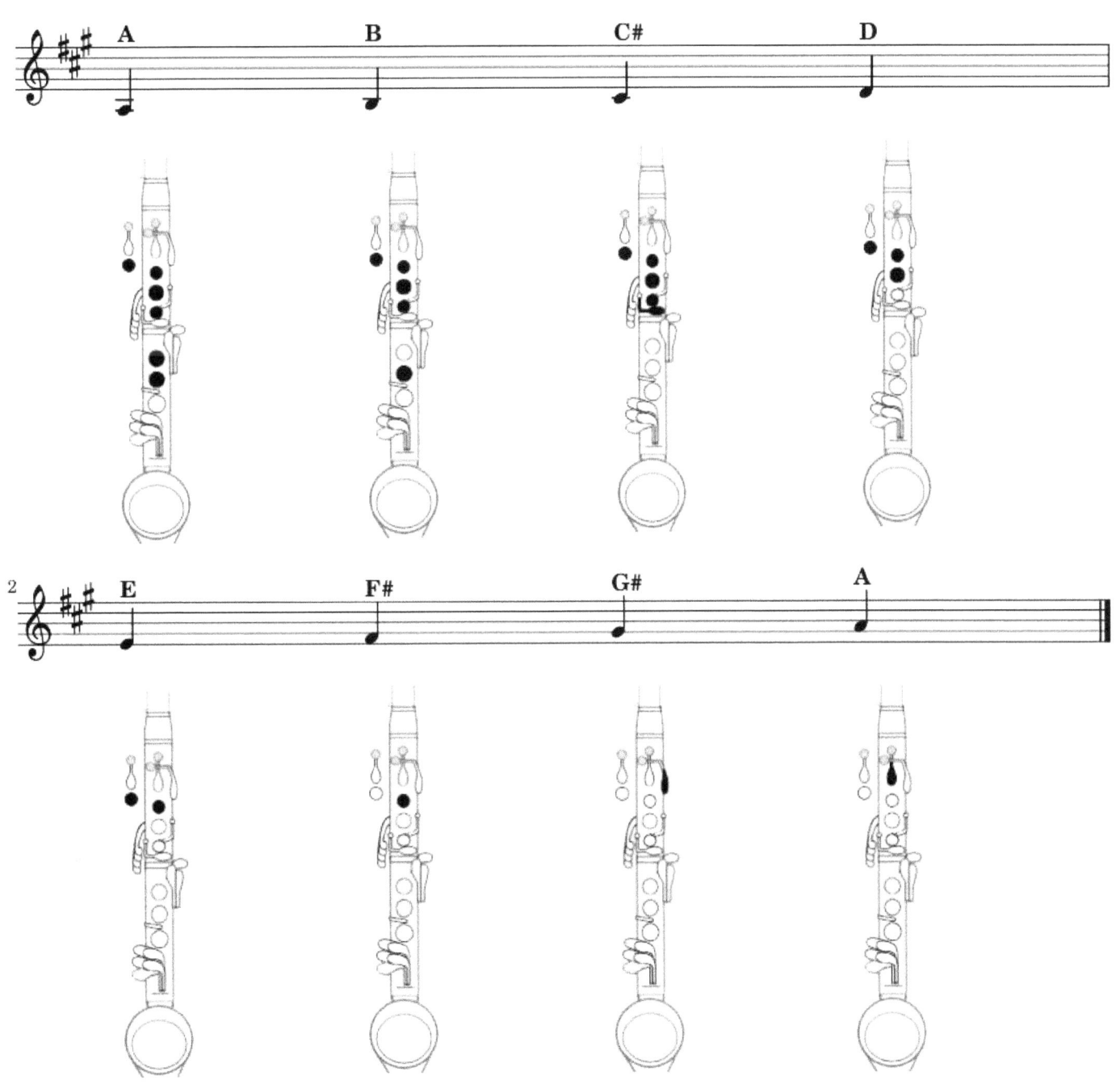

A Major Scale Descending

How about the A major scale higher octave descending? This one really gives your fingers a workout. You've got this!

Remember, each note comes with a fingering diagram showing you which keys to press.

- Black circles mean you should press those keys.
- Open circles mean those key cups stay untouched.
- Black keys mean you press those keys.

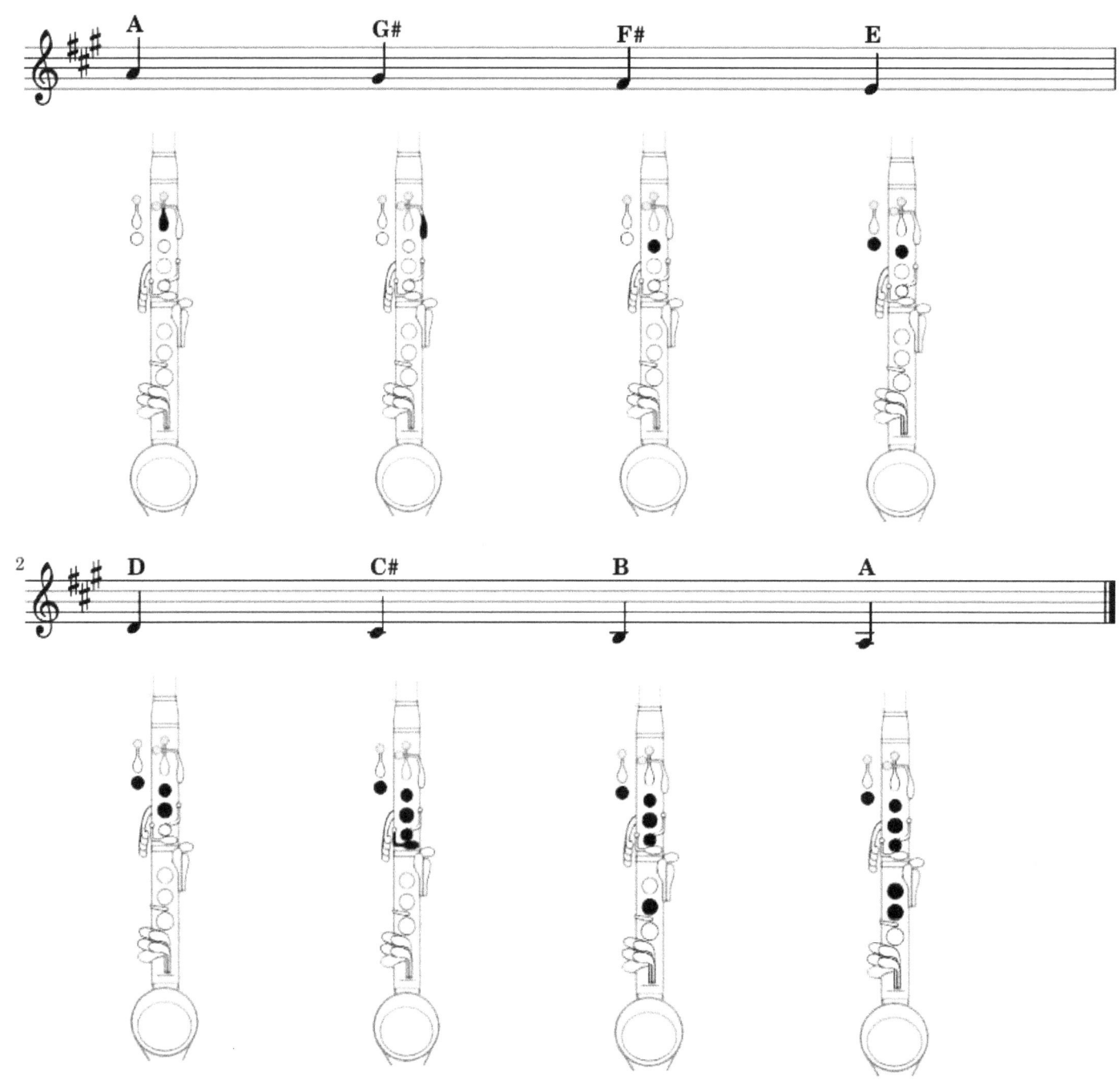

What is Your Embouchure?

em·bou·chure | \ ˌäm-bü-ˈshu̇r

The embouchure is how a musician shapes and positions their lips, mouth, and facial muscles to control the sound and tone of a wind instrument, such as an alto clarinet. It is a delicate balance of muscle coordination and pressure that transforms air into music, acting as the "control panel" for sound quality, pitch, and projection on a wind instrument.

Your embouchure is how you use your lips, teeth, and mouth to play the clarinet, and it makes a big difference in how you sound. Let's talk about how to balance the pressure you use so your playing feels easier and your sound improves.

What Is Embouchure Pressure?
Think of your reed, lips, and teeth as a team working together to make music. If one part isn't doing its job, or if it's working too hard, it can mess things up.

Too much pressure: Your sound might become thin or squeaky.
Too little pressure: The sound could get airy or weak.

The goal is to find just the right amount of pressure so your reed vibrates freely, and you can produce a steady, warm tone.

How do you know if something's not quite right? Listen to your sound.

Squeaks: Your reed might not be vibrating evenly because of uneven pressure.
Breathy sound: This happens if your lips aren't sealing well around the mouthpiece.
Tired mouth muscles: You might be pressing too hard or using muscles that don't need to work as much.

> **Tips to Improve Your Embouchure**
>
> Bottom Lip: Roll it over your teeth to cushion the reed. No biting.
>
> Top Teeth: Rest them lightly on the mouthpiece for stability.
>
> Lip Shape: Form an "O" around the mouthpiece for a focused, airtight seal.

Playing Tips

Tips to Improve Your Embouchure
Bottom Lip Placement: Roll your bottom lip slightly over your bottom teeth to create a cushion for the reed. Don't press or bite down hard.
Top Teeth Placement: Rest your top teeth lightly on the mouthpiece. Just enough to keep the clarinet steady. No biting.
Form a Round Shape: Imagine your lips making an "O" around the mouthpiece. This helps you seal the air and keep the sound focused.
Reed Strength: Softer reeds are easier to play, while harder reeds might need a little more control. Experiment to find what works for you. A #2 reed is a good place to start.

Practice Makes Perfect
Try this simple exercise to improve your embouchure:

Long Tones: Play one note for as long as you can. Focus on keeping the sound steady and smooth. Pay attention to how your lips feel and adjust if the tone sounds uneven.
When you hear squeaks (yes! we all squeek sometimes while learning) or your tone sounds breathy, don't worry, it's just your clarinet telling you to make a slight change. Adjust your lips and pressure until your sound improves.

Using the Right Equipment
A good clarinet setup can make everything easier. Check your mouthpiece and reed to make sure they fit well together. If you're not sure, ask your teacher or someone at your local music store for advice.

Keep It Fun!
Remember, playing the clarinet is about more than just technique, it's about making music and having fun. Take your time to improve, and don't get frustrated if things don't sound perfect right away. Enjoy the process, and before you know it, playing will feel natural and sound amazing!

Check your mouthpiece and reed to make sure they fit well together.

E Major Scale (Low)

Let's investigate the E major scale (low). You know what to do!

Remember, each note comes with a fingering diagram showing you which keys to press.

- Black circles mean you should press those keys.
- Open circles mean those key cups stay untouched.
- Black keys mean you press those keys.

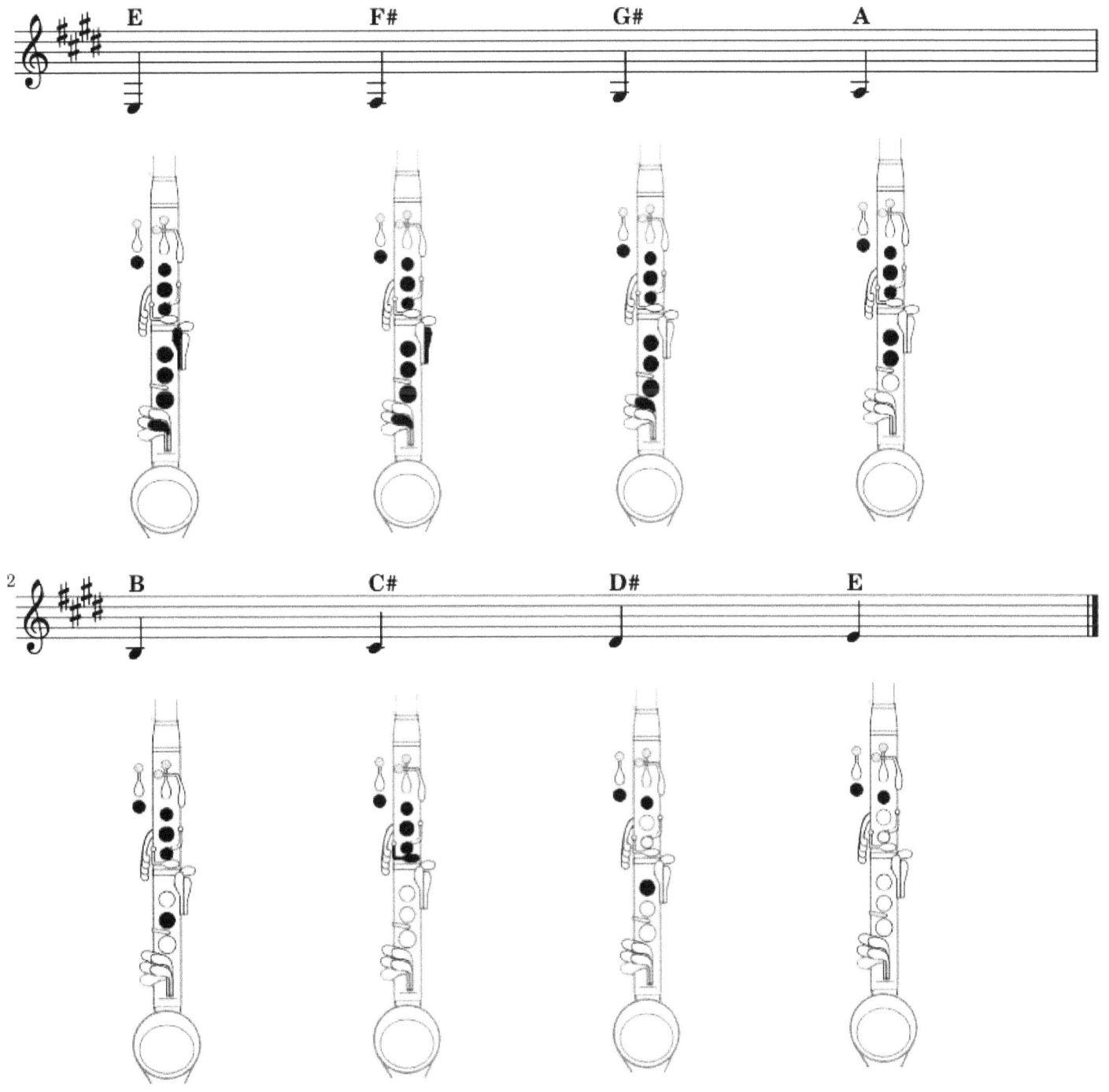

E Major Scale (Higher)

Let's get into the E major scale higher octave. Watch out for that A note to B note register jump!

Remember, each note comes with a fingering diagram showing you which keys to press.

 - Black circles mean you should press those keys.
 - Open circles mean those key cups stay untouched.
 - Black keys mean you press those keys.

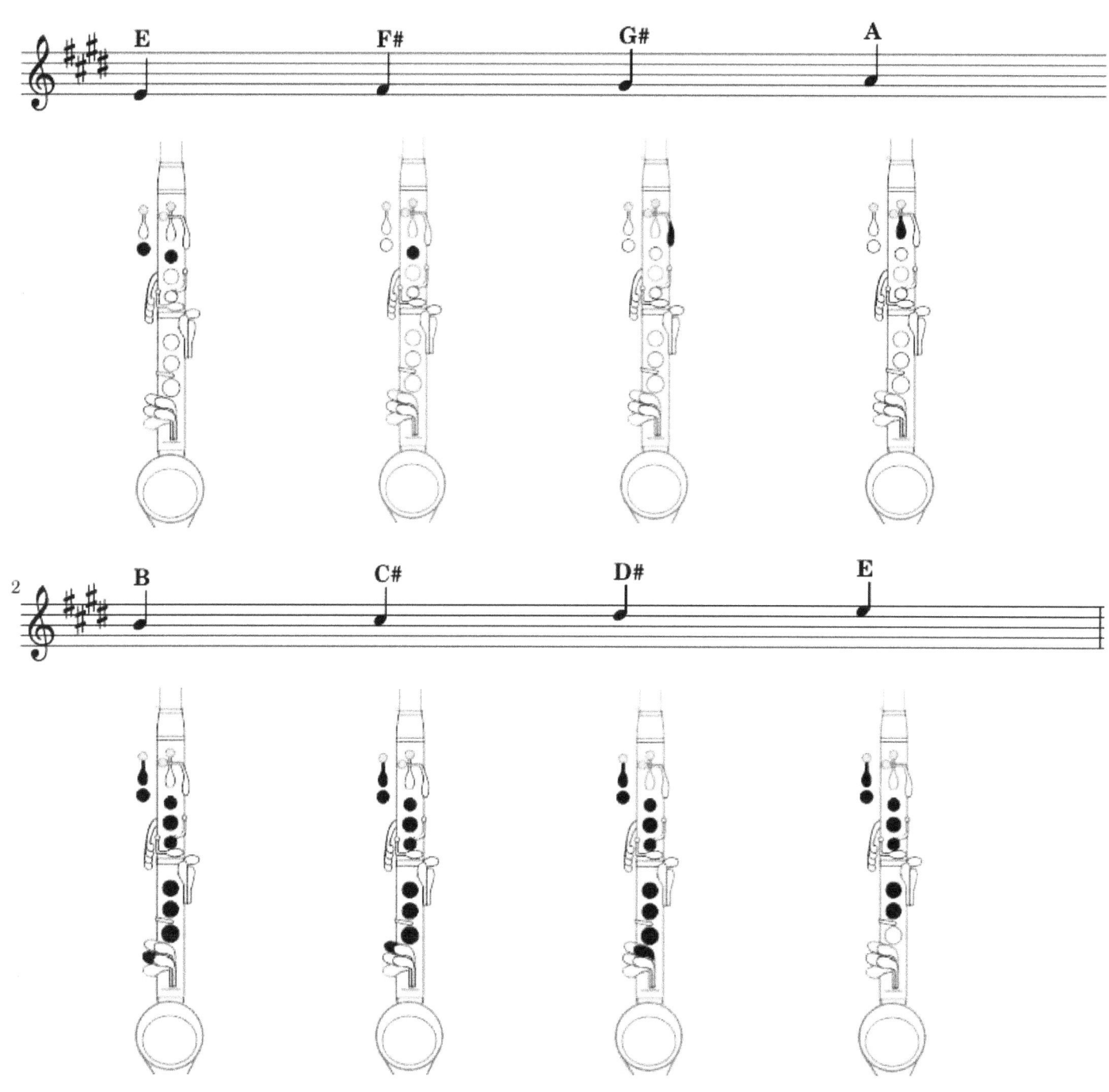

E♭ Major Scale (Low)

Let's flatten the E and work on the E♭ major scale ascending. This scale begins with the lowest note on an E♭ alto clarinet. Practice, practice, practice those pinky keys!

Remember, each note comes with a fingering diagram showing you which keys to press.

- Black circles mean you should press those keys.
- Open circles mean those key cups stay untouched.
- Black keys mean you press those keys.

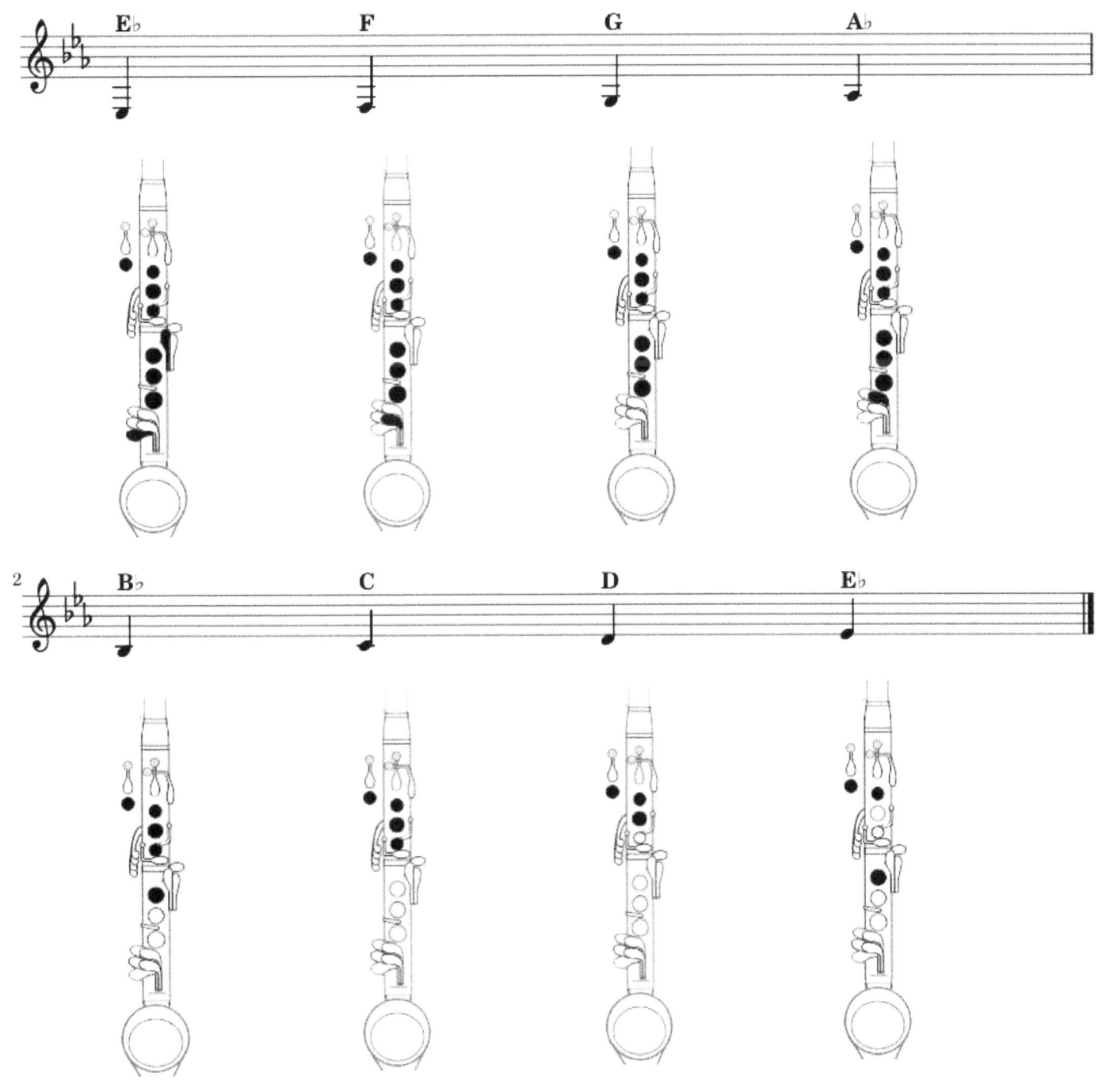

E♭ Major Scale (Higher)

Let's work on the E♭ major scale in a higher register. Did you know that E♭ and D# are the same fingering and same tone? See the E♭ alto clarinet fingering chart beginning on page 61.

Remember, each note comes with a fingering diagram showing you which keys to press.

- Black circles mean you should press those keys.
- Open circles mean those key cups stay untouched.
- Black keys mean you press those keys.

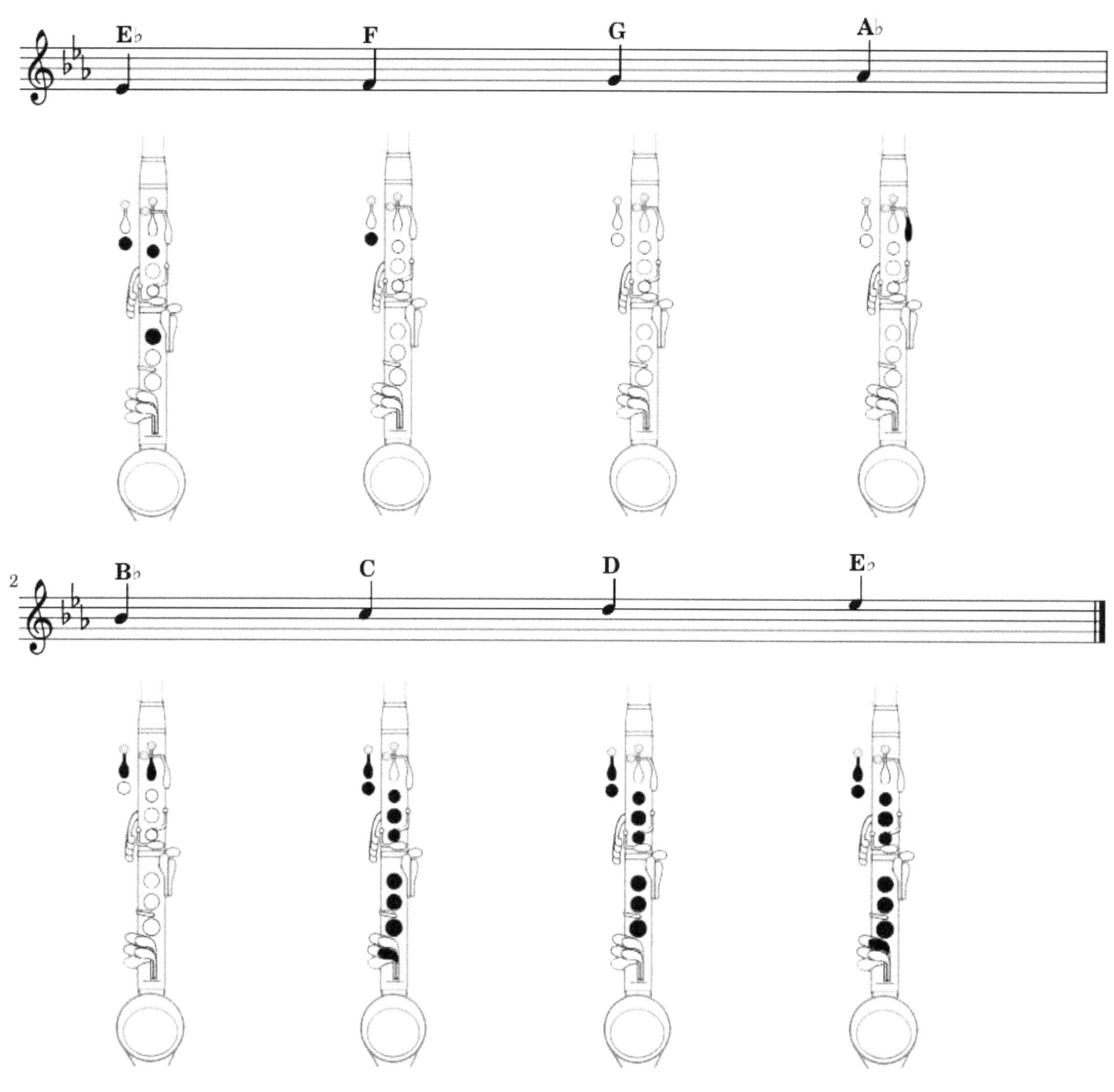

B Major Scale Ascending

It's time for the B major scale ascending. Watch out for the tricky pinky zone keys!

Remember, each note comes with a fingering diagram showing you which keys to press.

- Black circles mean you should press those keys.
- Open circles mean those key cups stay untouched.
- Black keys mean you press those keys.

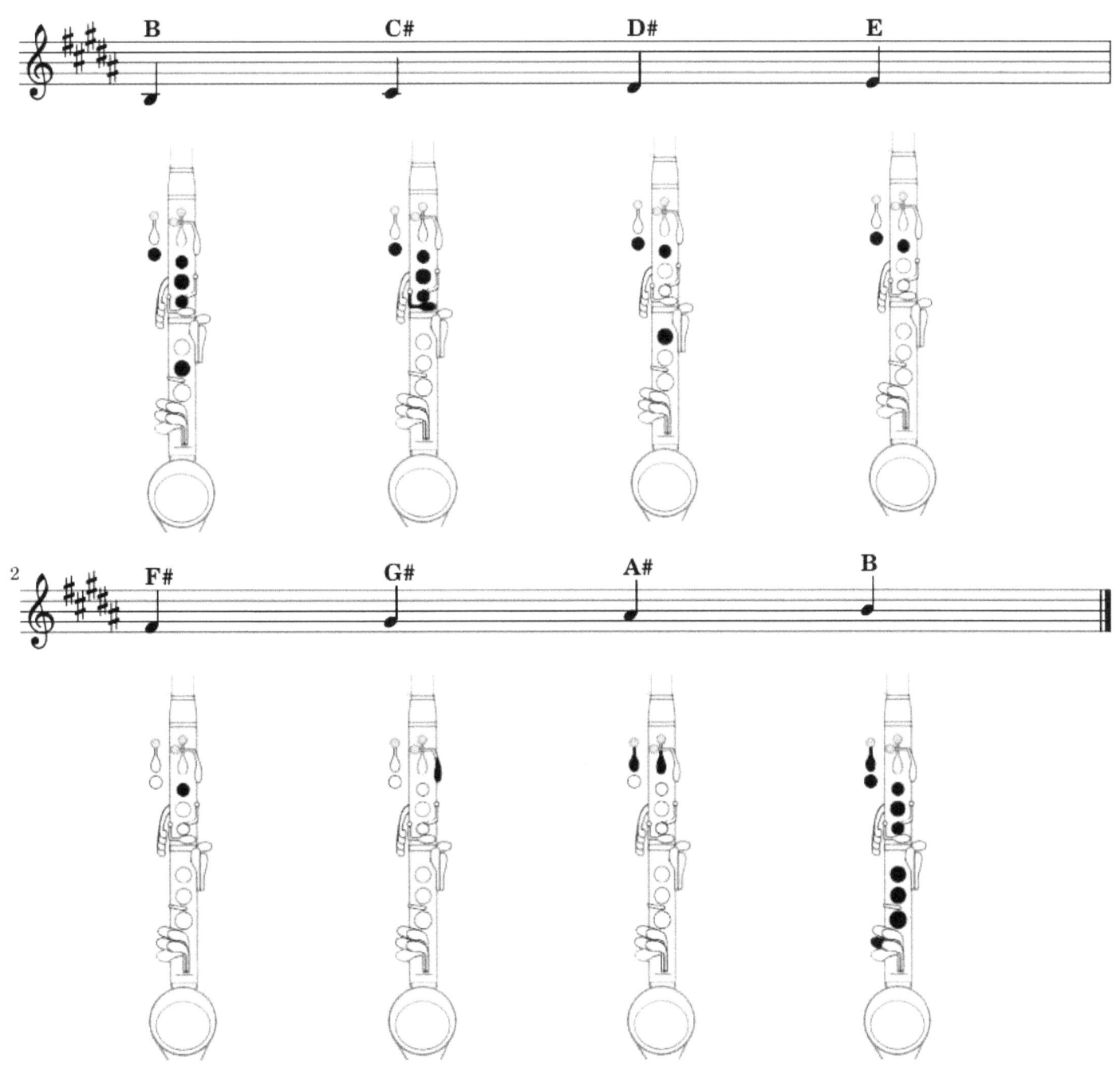

B Major Scale Descending

It's time for the B major scale descending. You've got this!

Remember, each note comes with a fingering diagram showing you which keys to press.

- Black circles mean you should press those keys.
- Open circles mean those key cups stay untouched.
- Black keys mean you press those keys.

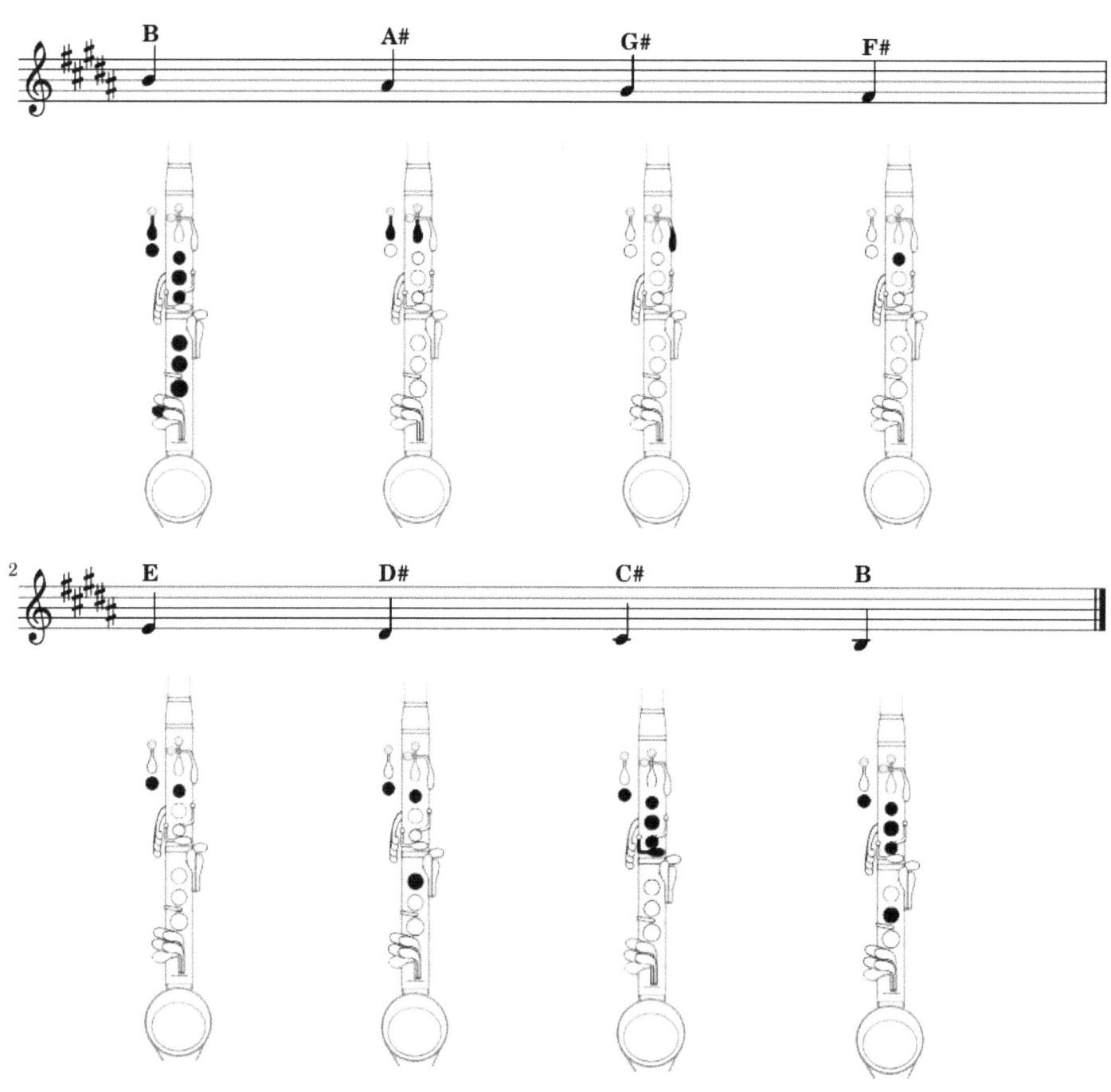

A♭ Major Scale Ascending

It's time for the A♭ major scale ascending. Take it nice and easy.

Remember, each note comes with a fingering diagram showing you which keys to press.

- Black circles mean you should press those keys.
- Open circles mean those key cups stay untouched.
- Black keys mean you press those keys.

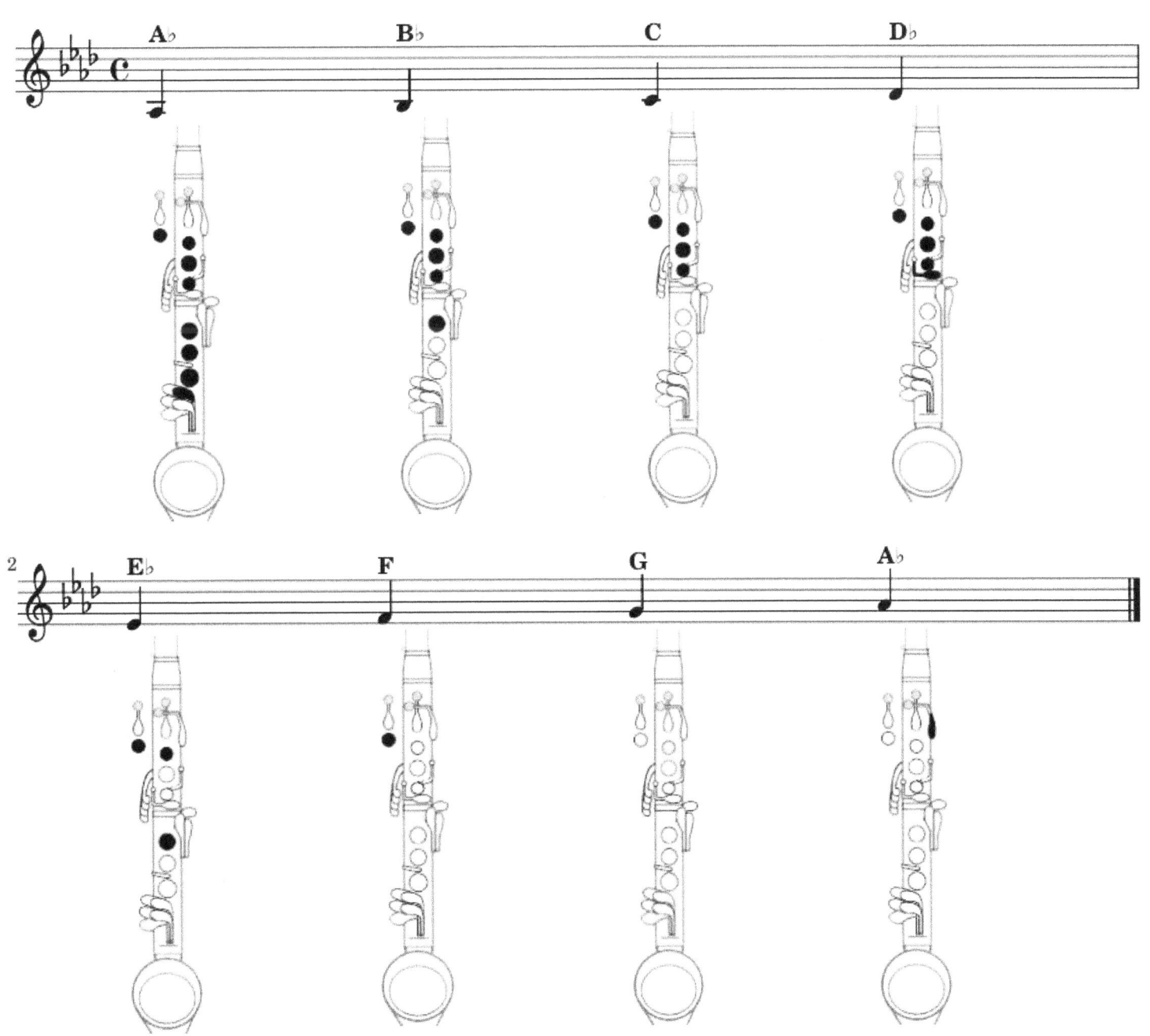

A♭ Major Scale Descending

It's time for the A♭ major scale descending. There are those pinky keys again!

Remember, each note comes with a fingering diagram showing you which keys to press.

- Black circles mean you should press those keys.
- Open circles mean those key cups stay untouched.
- Black keys mean you press those keys.

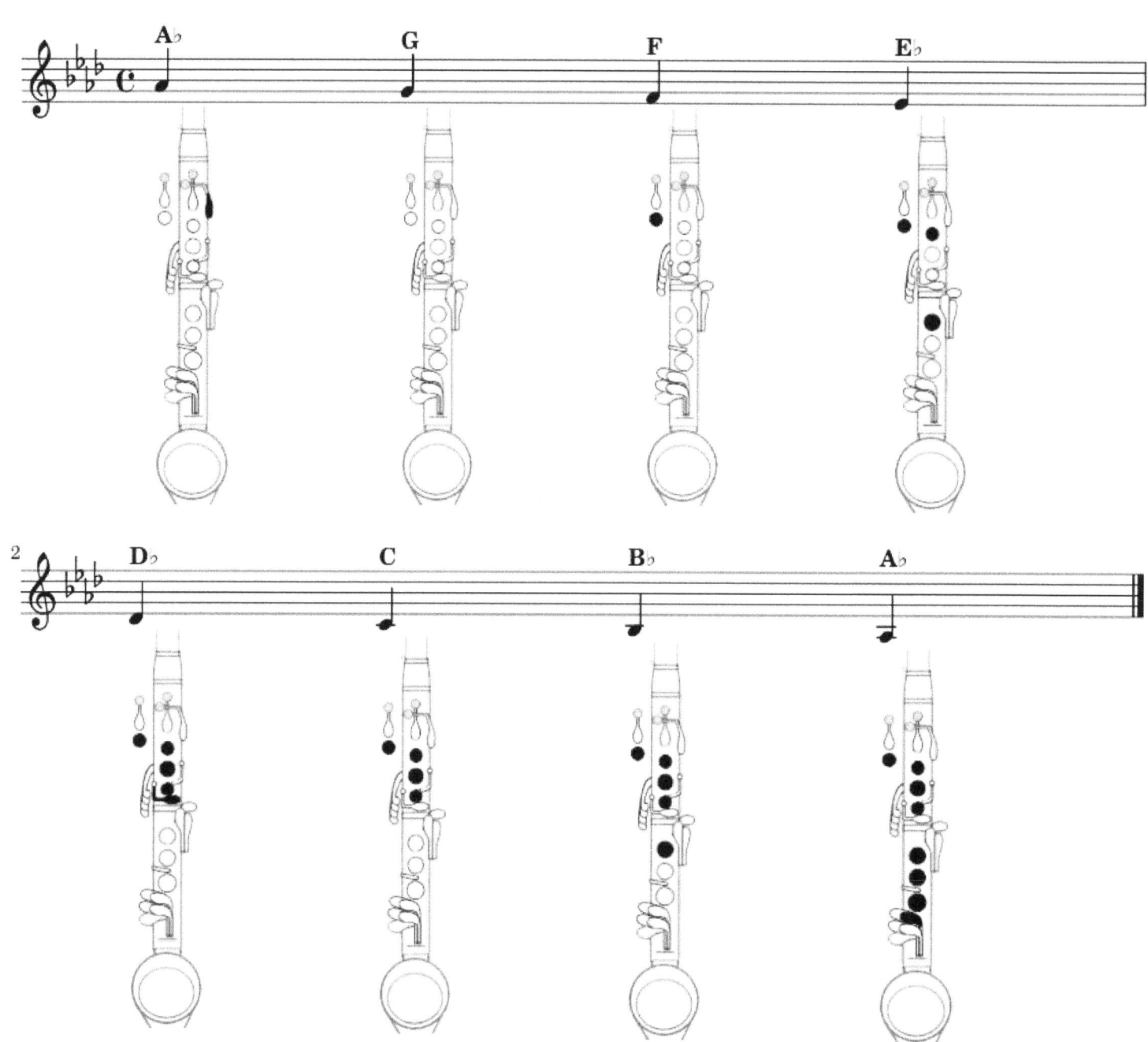

G♭ Major Scale (Low)

Let's work on the G♭ major scale in the lower octave. This first G♭ note can be tricky, so take your time. G♭ major includes the notes G♭, A♭, B♭, C♭, D♭, E♭, and F. The note C♭ is the same as the note B. How cool is that? See the E♭ alto clarinet fingering chart beginning on page 61.

Remember, each note comes with a fingering diagram showing you which keys to press.

   - Black circles mean you should press those keys.
   - Open circles mean those key cups stay untouched.
   - Black keys mean you press those keys.

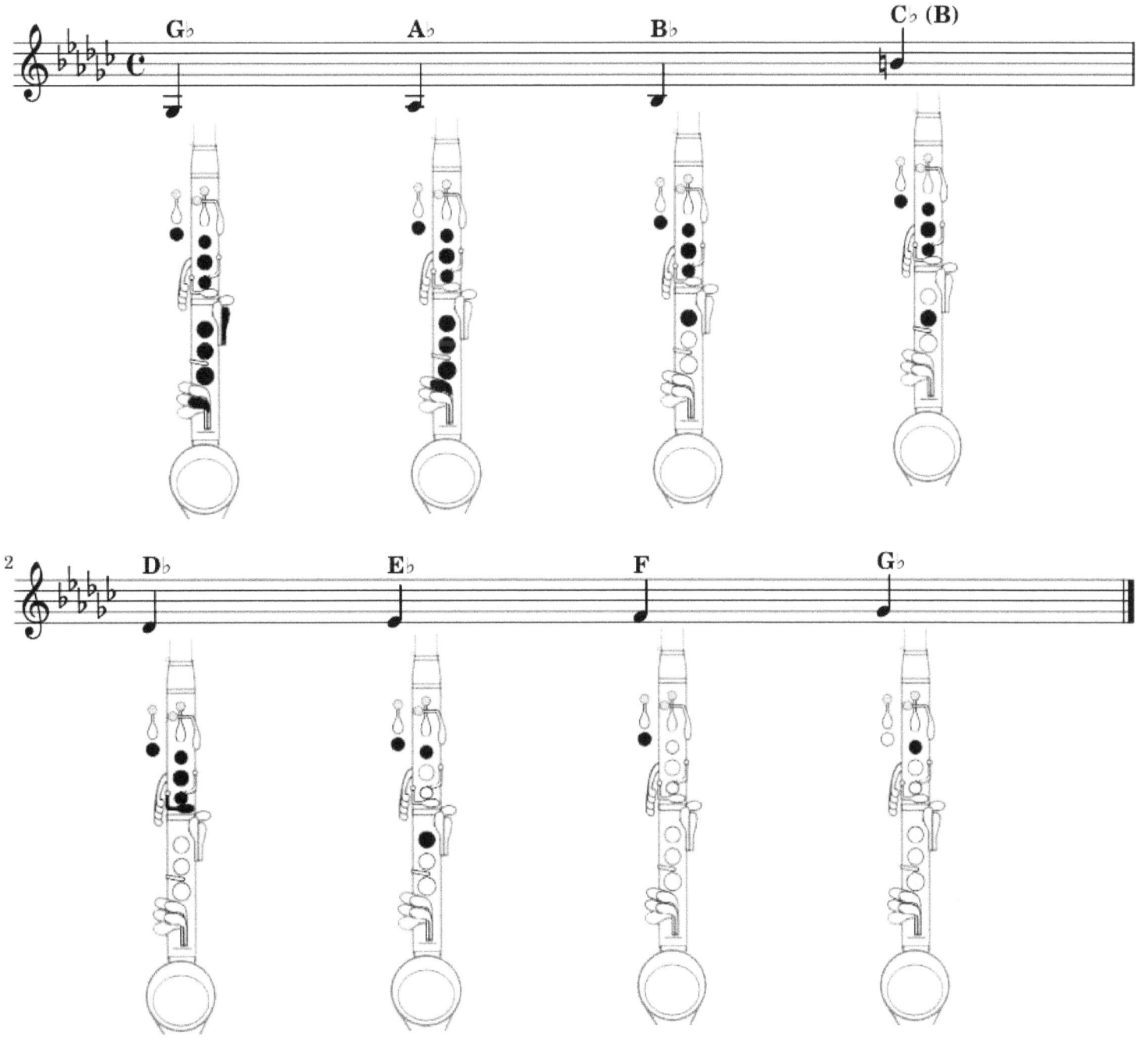

G♭ Major Scale (Higher)

Let's work on the G♭ major scale ascending in the higher octave. See the E♭ alto clarinet fingering chart beginning on page 61.

Remember, each note comes with a fingering diagram showing you which keys to press.

- Black circles mean you should press those keys.
- Open circles mean those key cups stay untouched.
- Black keys mean you press those keys.

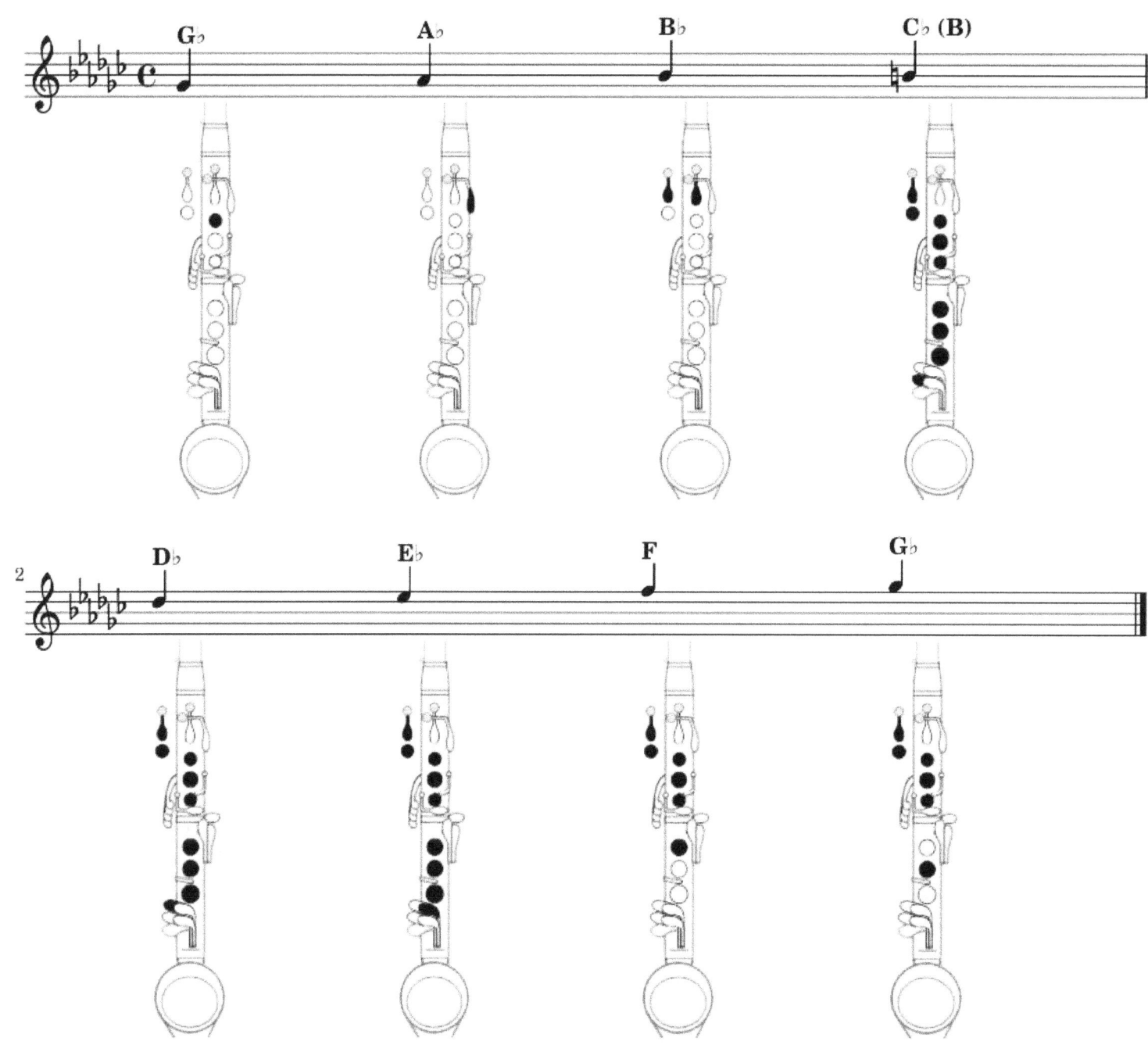

D♭ Major Scale Ascending

Let's work on the D♭ major scale ascending. The D♭ major scale includes the notes D♭, E♭, F, G♭, A♭, B♭, and C. Watch out for that big change!

Remember, each note comes with a fingering diagram showing you which keys to press.

- Black circles mean you should press those keys.
- Open circles mean those key cups stay untouched.
- Black keys mean you press those keys.

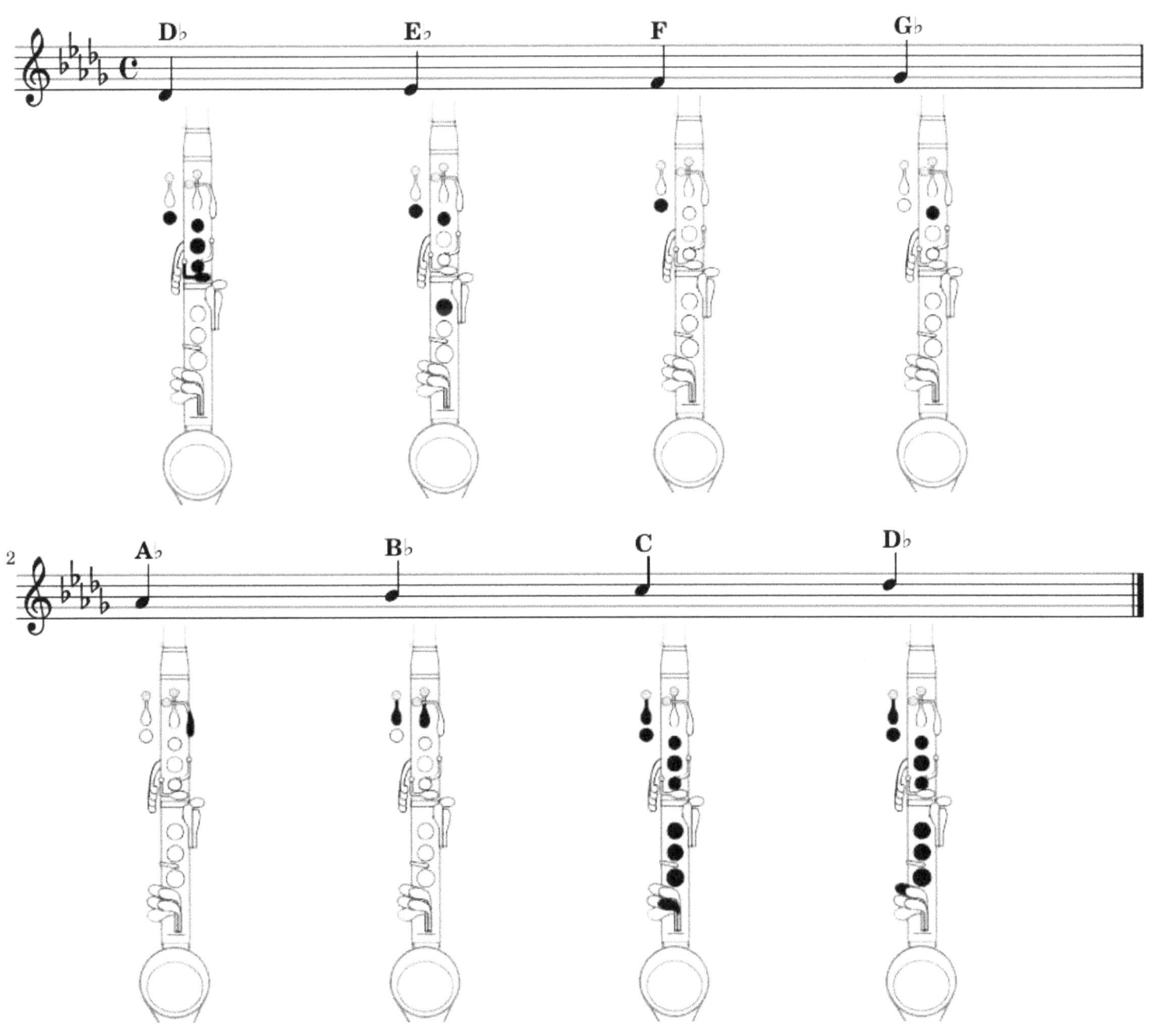

D♭ Major Scale Descending

Let's work on the D♭ major scale descending. Take it slowly.

Remember, each note comes with a fingering diagram showing you which keys to press.

- Black circles mean you should press those keys.
- Open circles mean those key cups stay untouched.
- Black keys mean you press those keys.

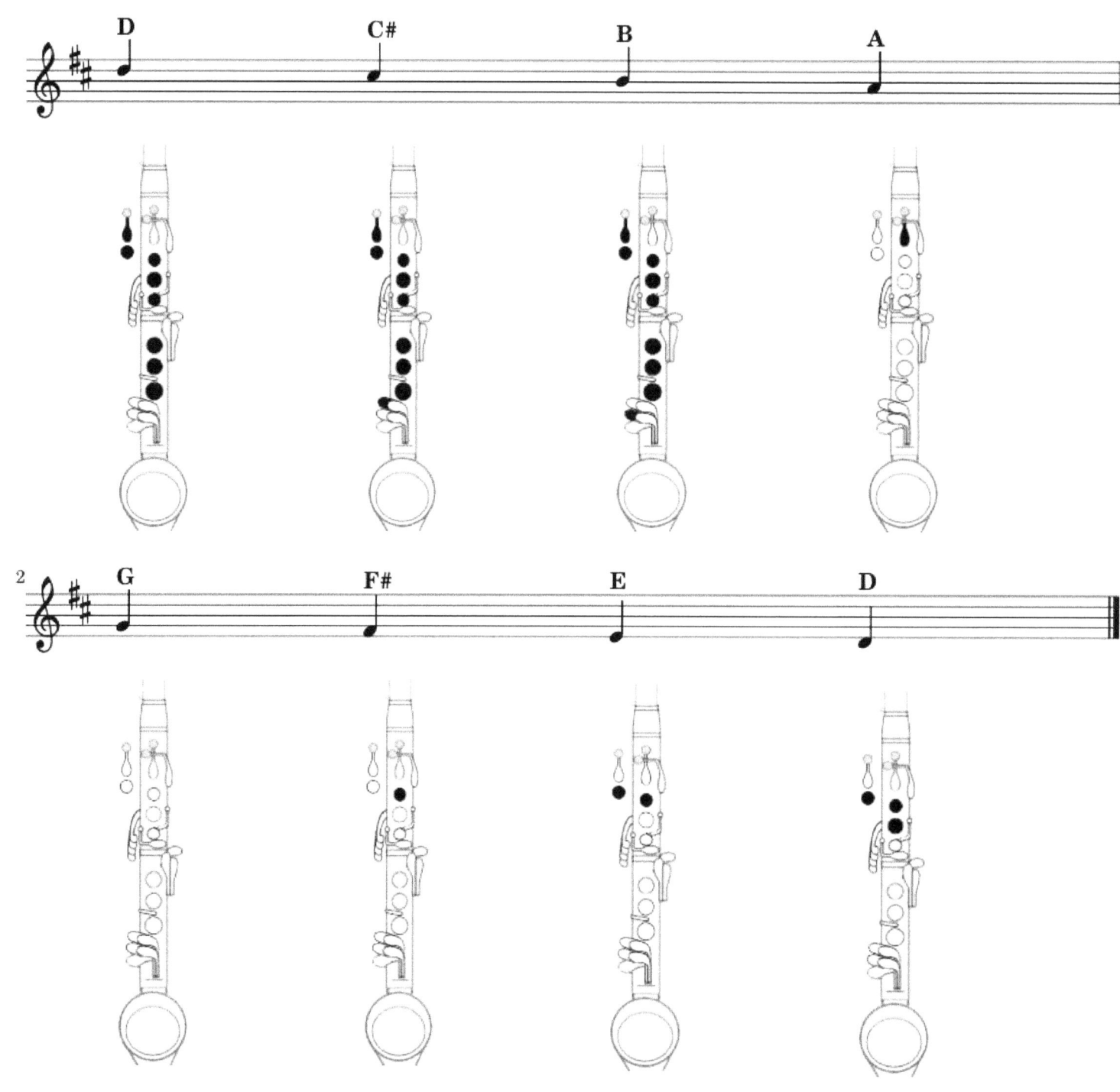

Chromatic Scale, E♭

Let's work on the Chromatic Scale. A chromatic scale is a musical scale that goes up or down by half steps, the smallest steps in music. Think of playing every single note in order, without skipping any. For this chromatic scale, we'll begin and end with E♭.

Remember, each note comes with a fingering diagram showing you which keys to press.

  - Black circles mean you should press those keys.
  - Open circles mean those key cups stay untouched.
  - Black keys mean you press those keys.

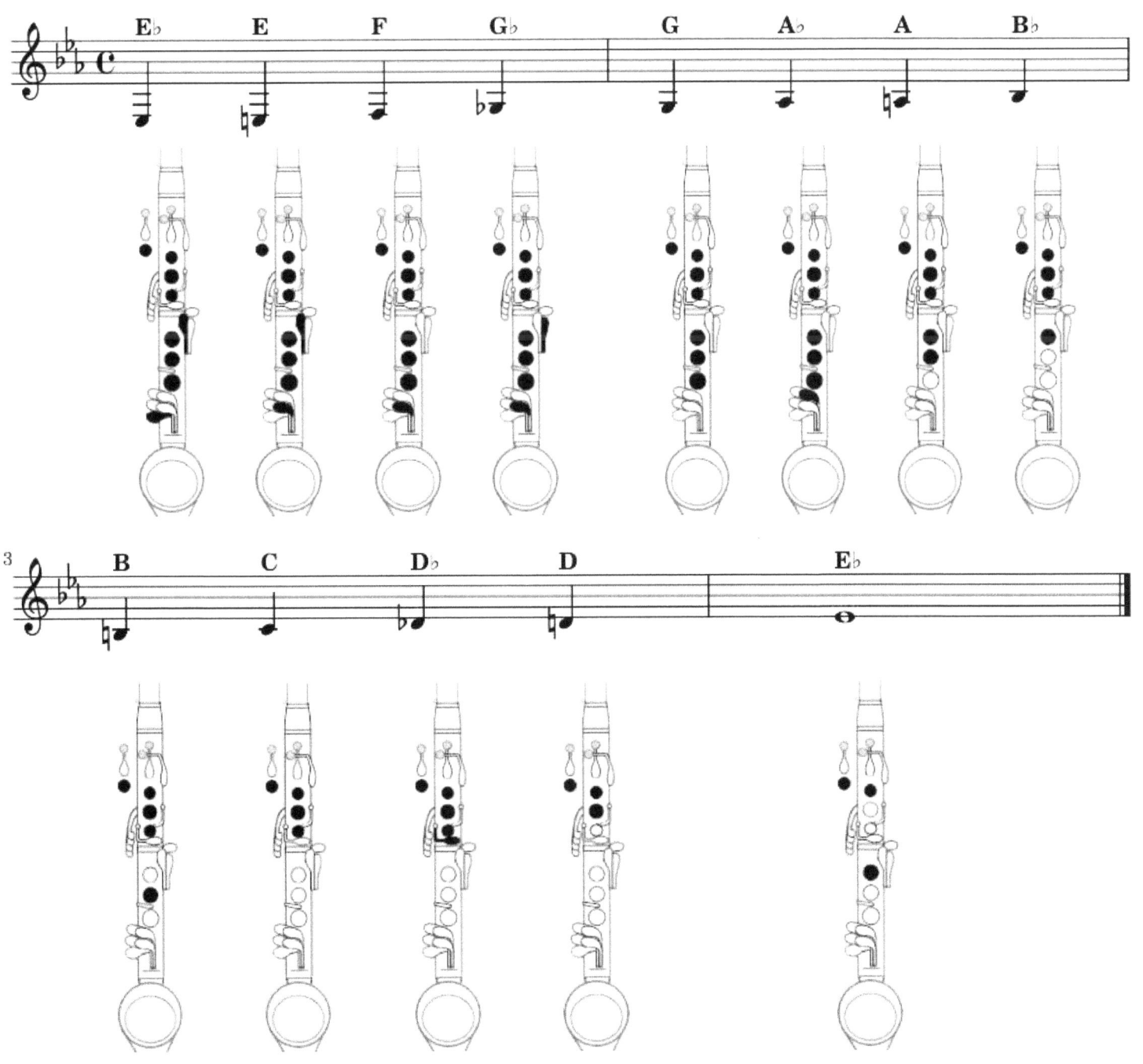

Mary Had a Little Lamb

Let's try a song we all know. Listen to the song first using the QR Code. Practice each note on its own. Then, practice moving from one note to the next. Go slowly at first. You've got this!

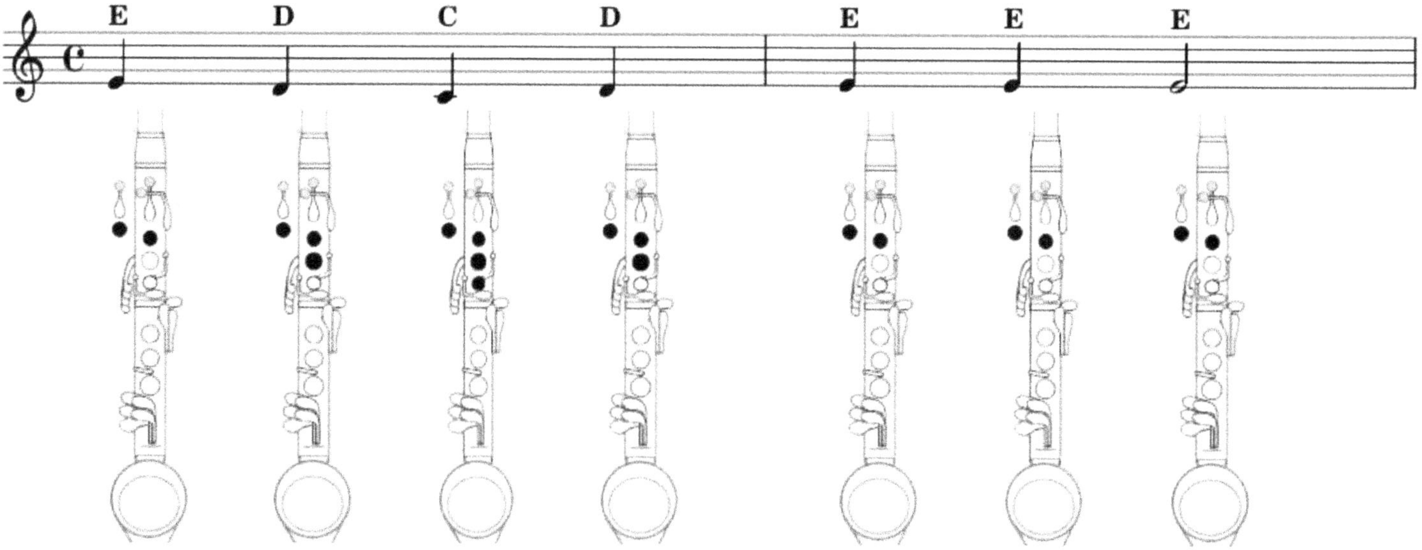

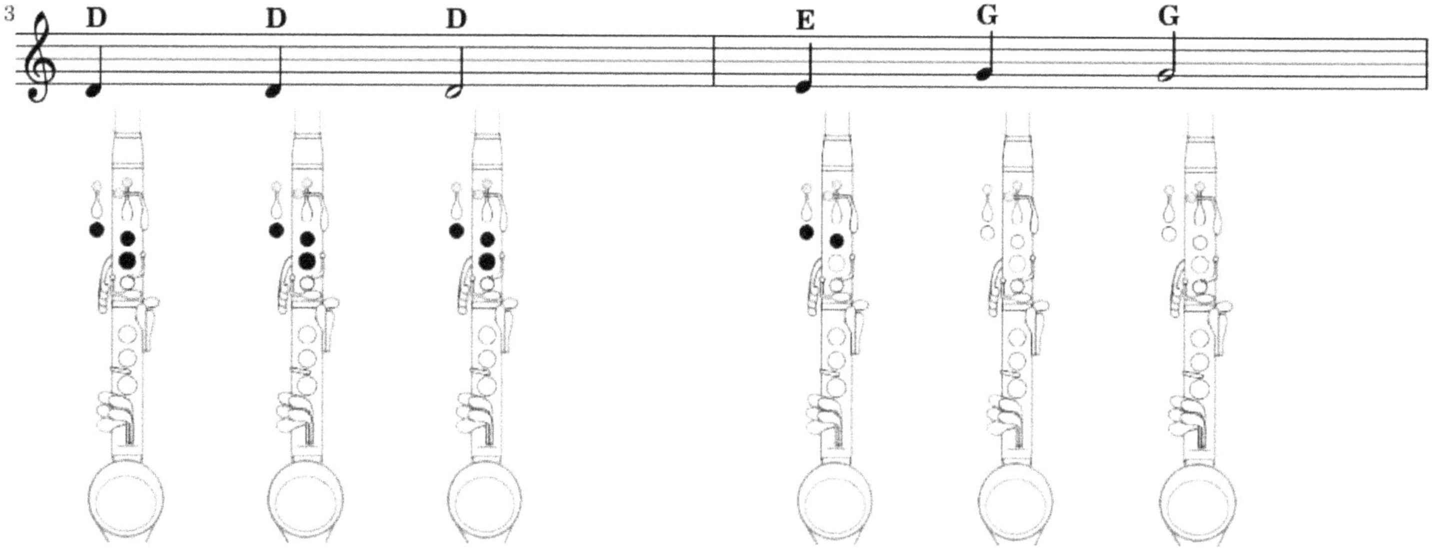

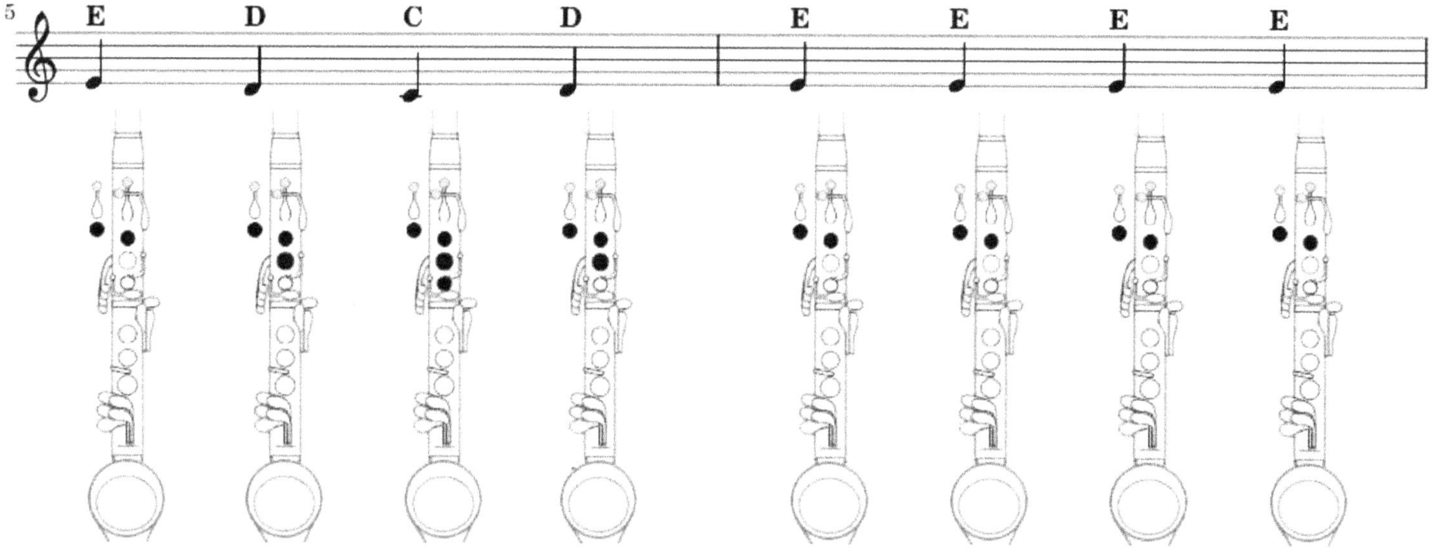

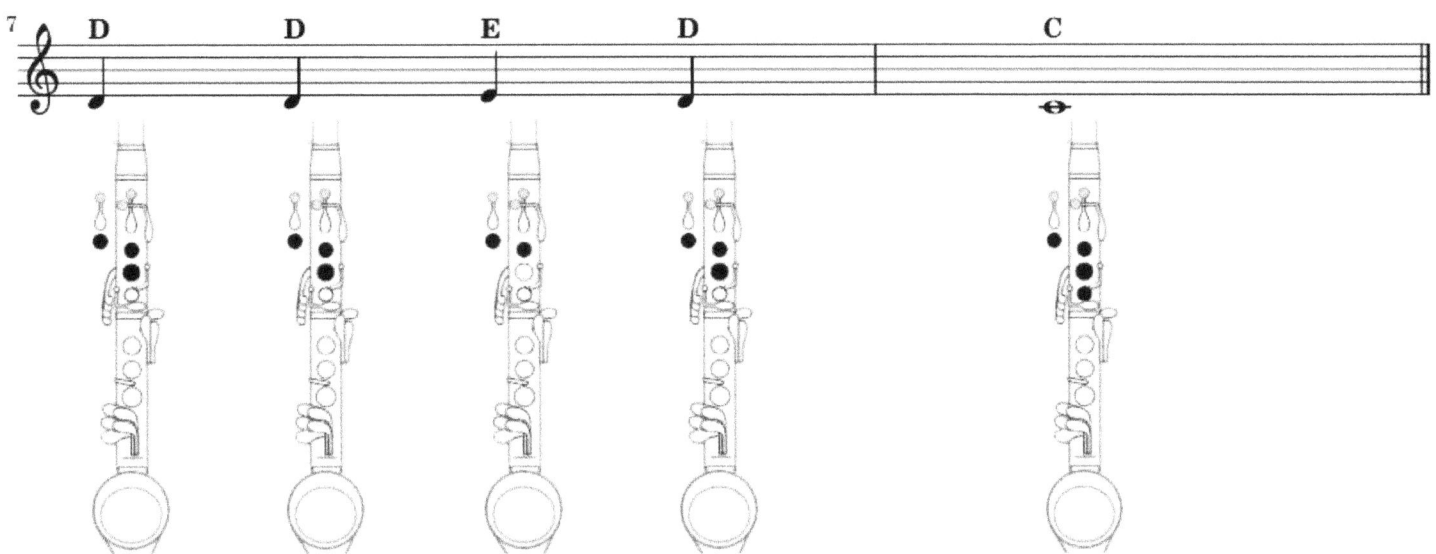

As the legend goes, this song was inspired by an actual event involving a girl named Mary Elizabeth Sawyer (1806–1889), who lived in Sterling, Massachusetts. According to Mary's writings, when she was a young girl, she nursed a sickly lamb back to health, and the lamb became attached to her. One day, the lamb followed Mary to school, creating a scene that amused her classmates and teacher.

Today, the Redstone Schoolhouse, where Mary's lamb supposedly followed her, is preserved as a historical site in Sudbury, Massachusetts, and continues to commemorate the tale.

Scan the QR Code

to Listen to the song!

☆ Twinkle Twinkle Little Star

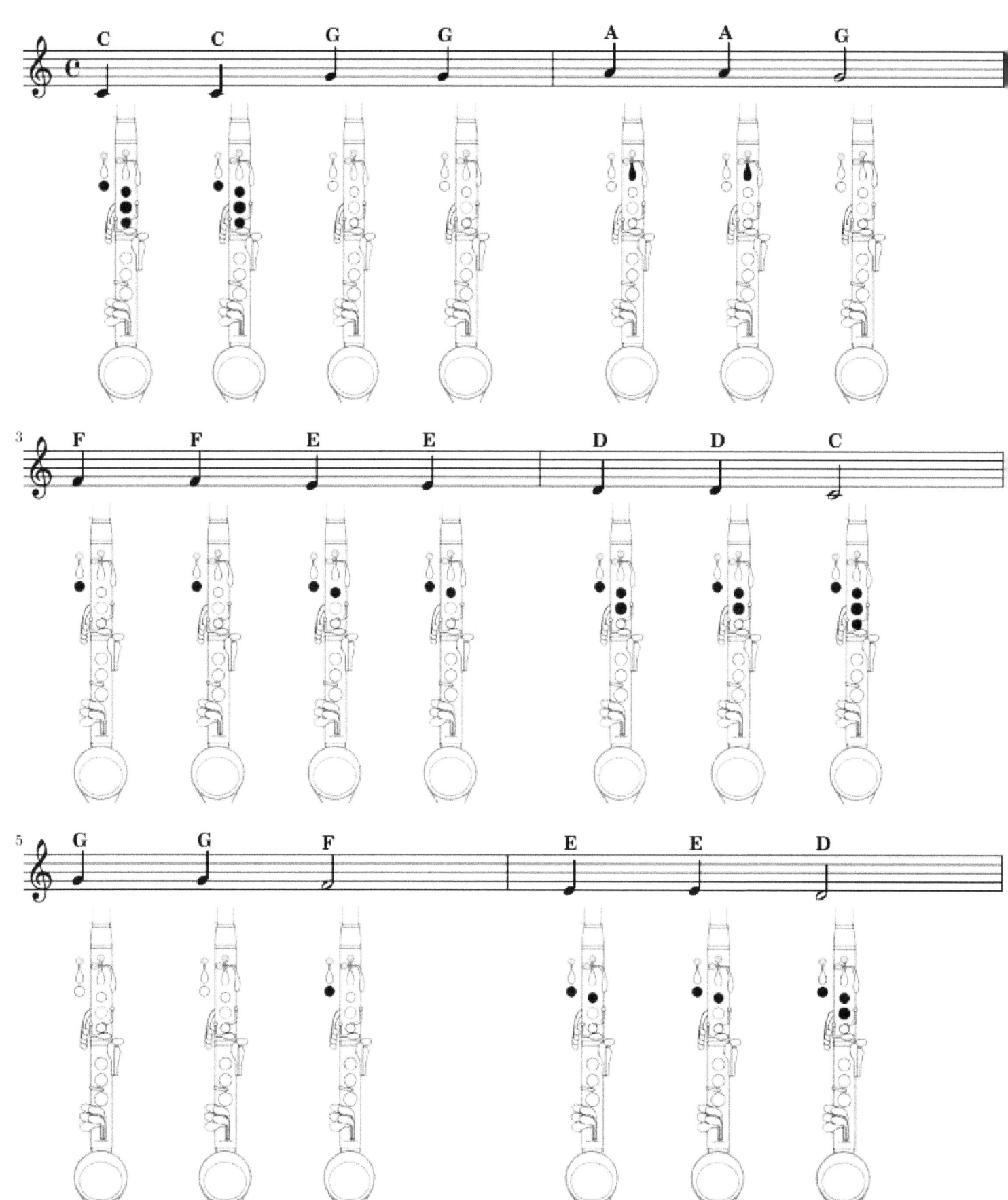

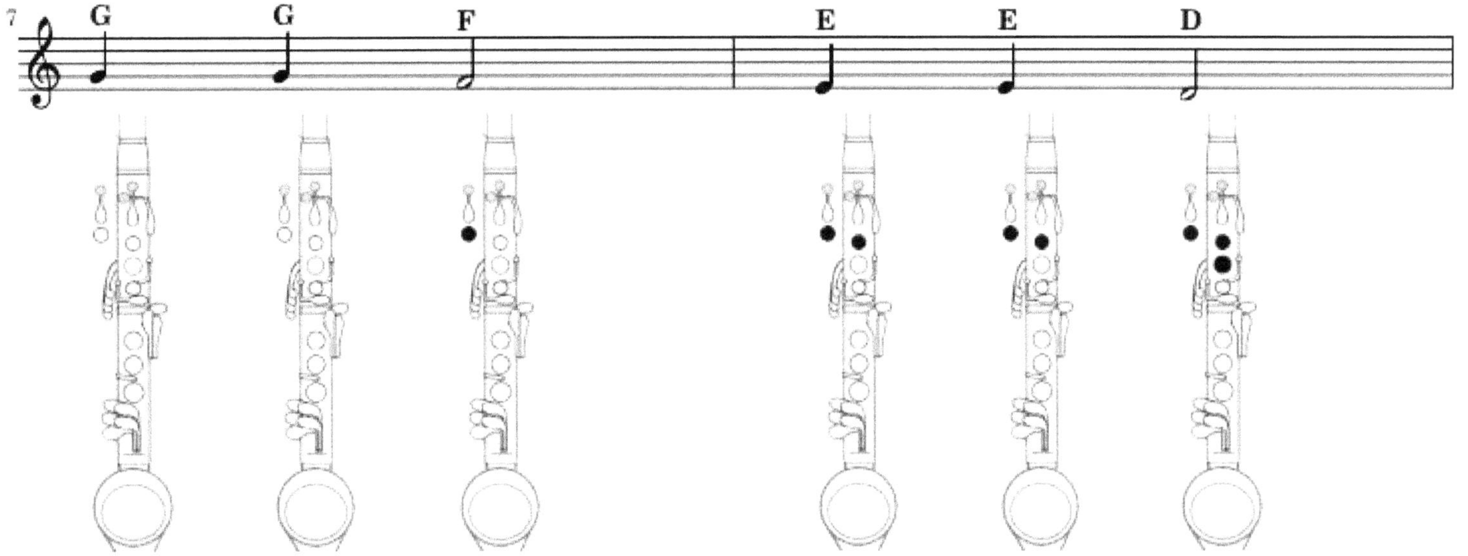

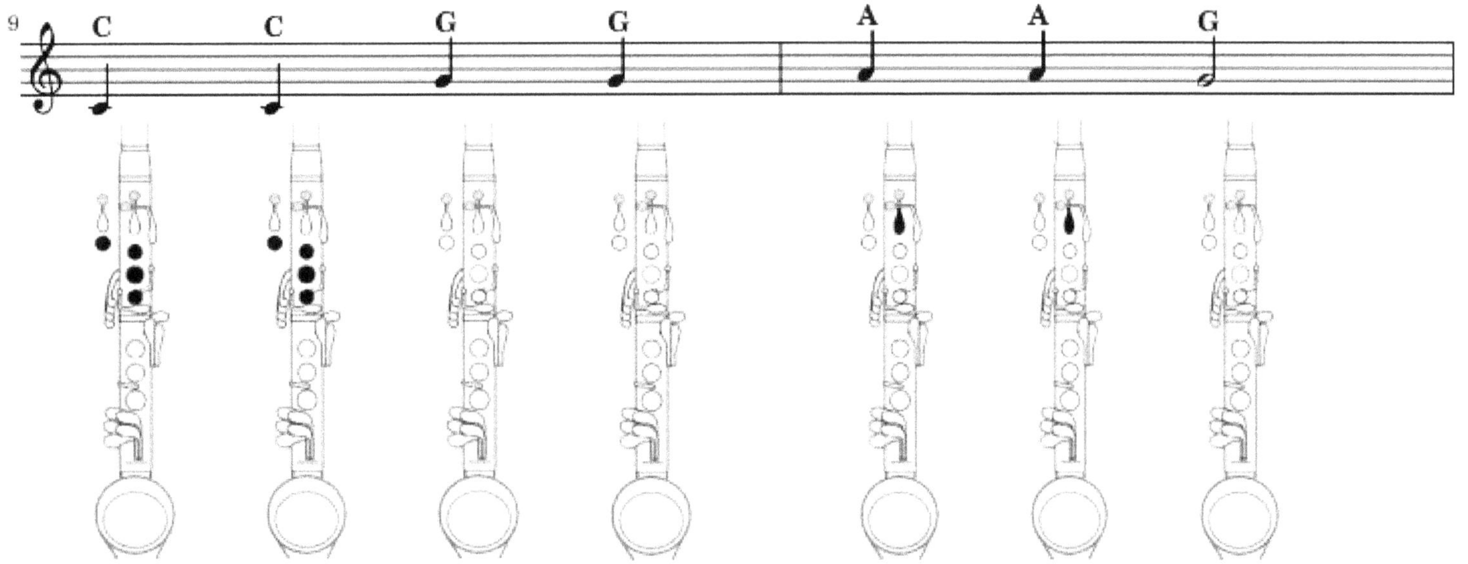

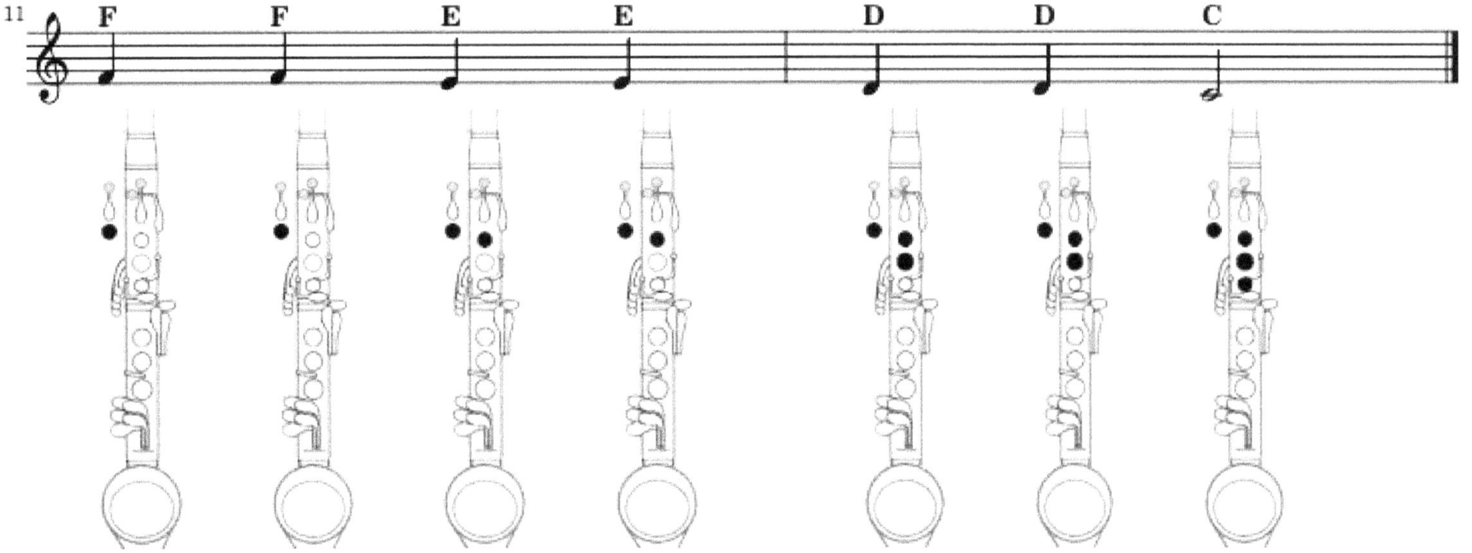

Scan the QR Code   Listen to the song!

Frère Jacques (Brother John)

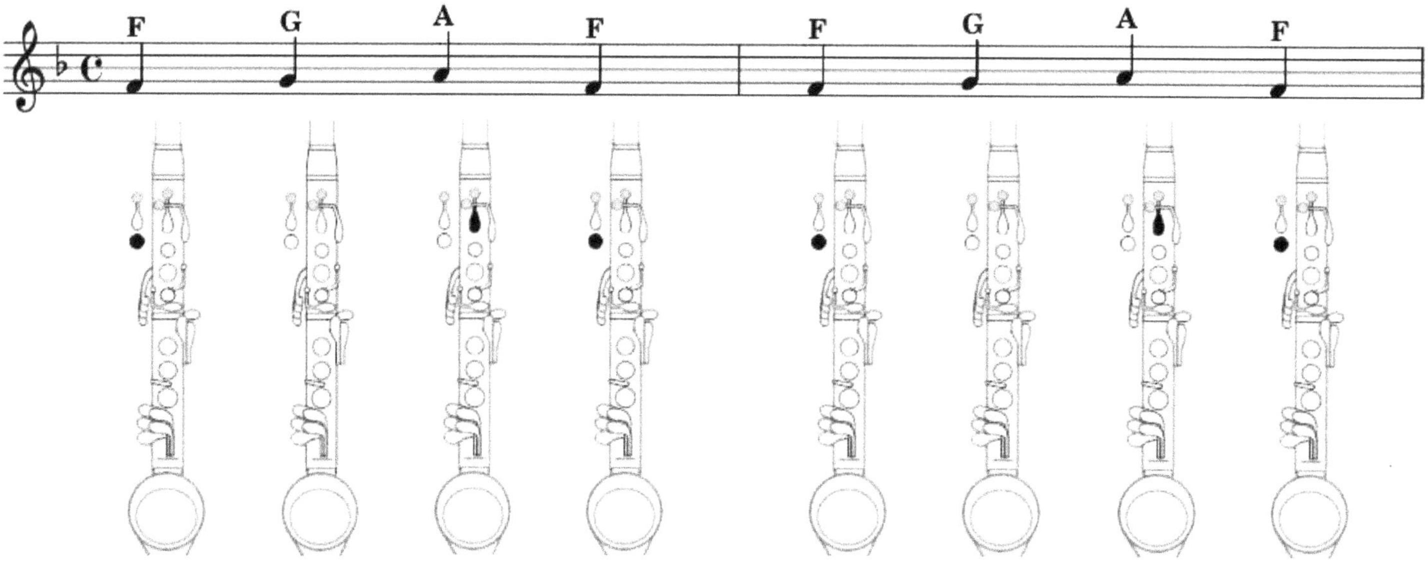

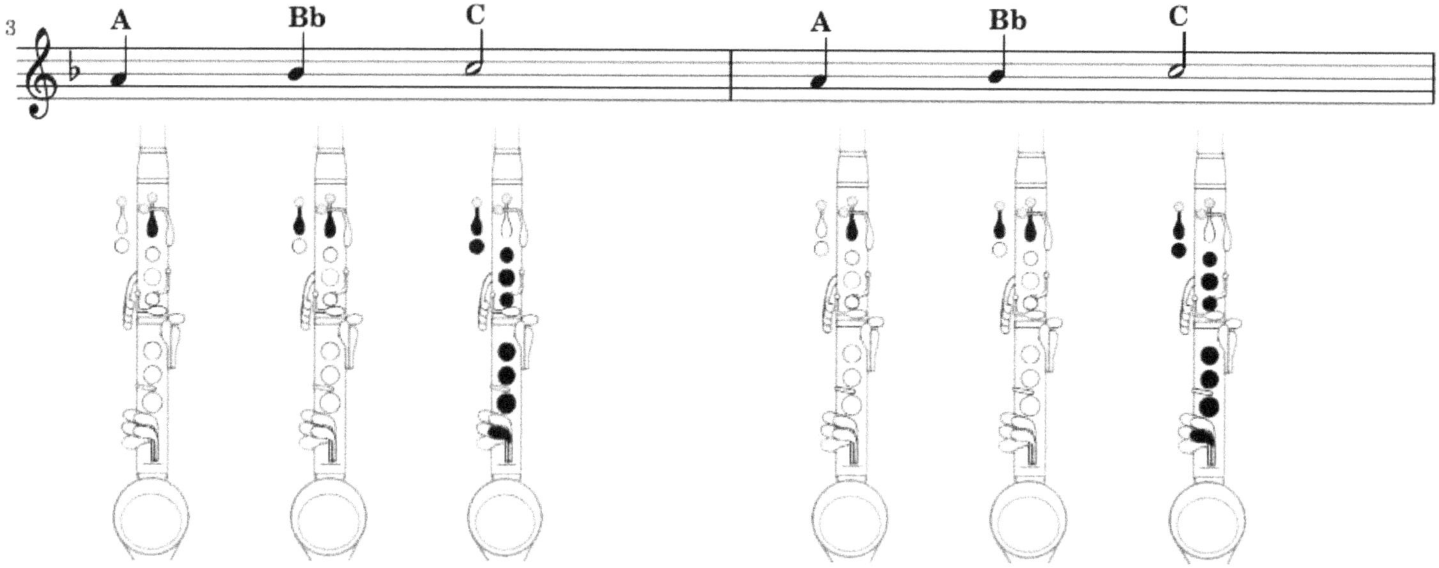

Big Change!

Big Change!

Going slowly, practice playing Bb to C to Bb to C to Bb seven times in a row. Keep your fingers close and your air steady. Soon you'll be able to make that big change without even thinking about it.

Scan the QR Code

to Listen to the song!

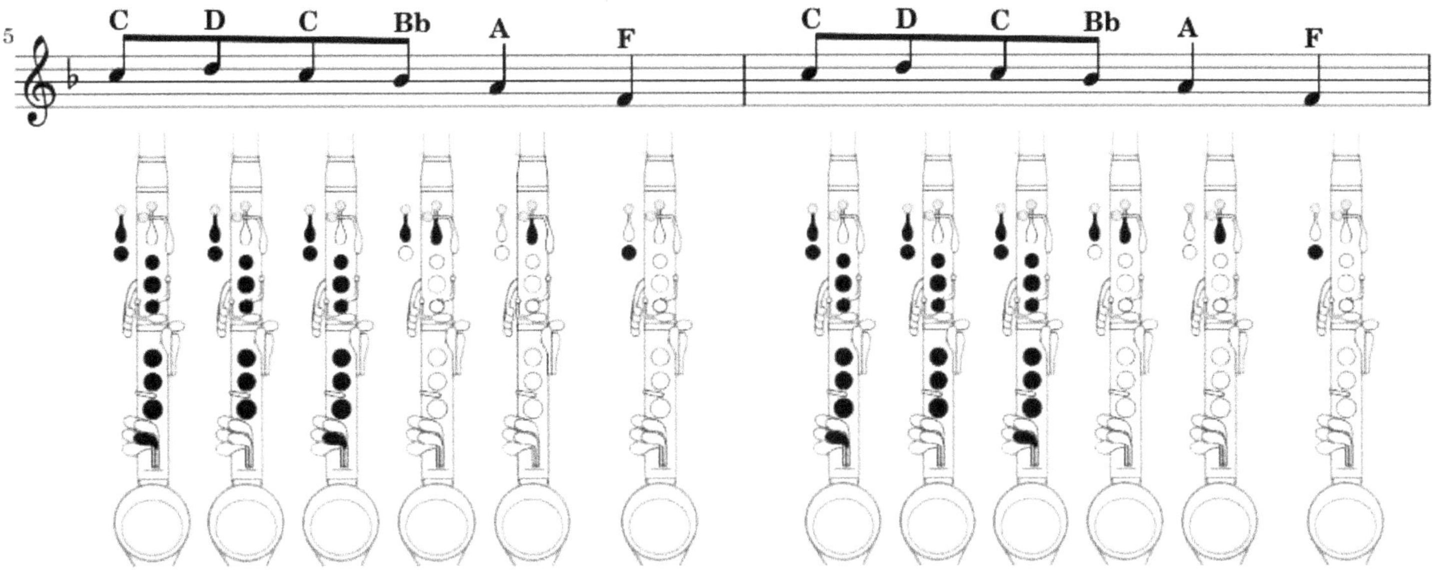

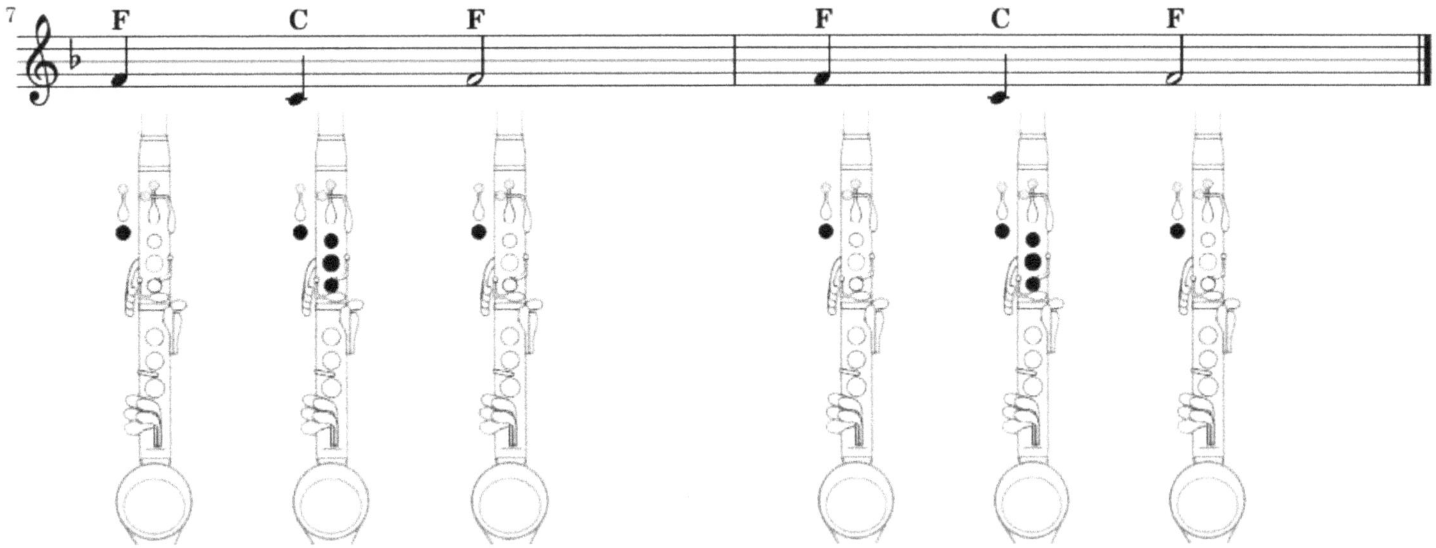

The song "Frère Jacques" is a traditional French nursery rhyme and song that dates back to at least the 18th century. Its simple, repetitive melody and lyrics have made it popular worldwide.

It's a Jazzy Day!

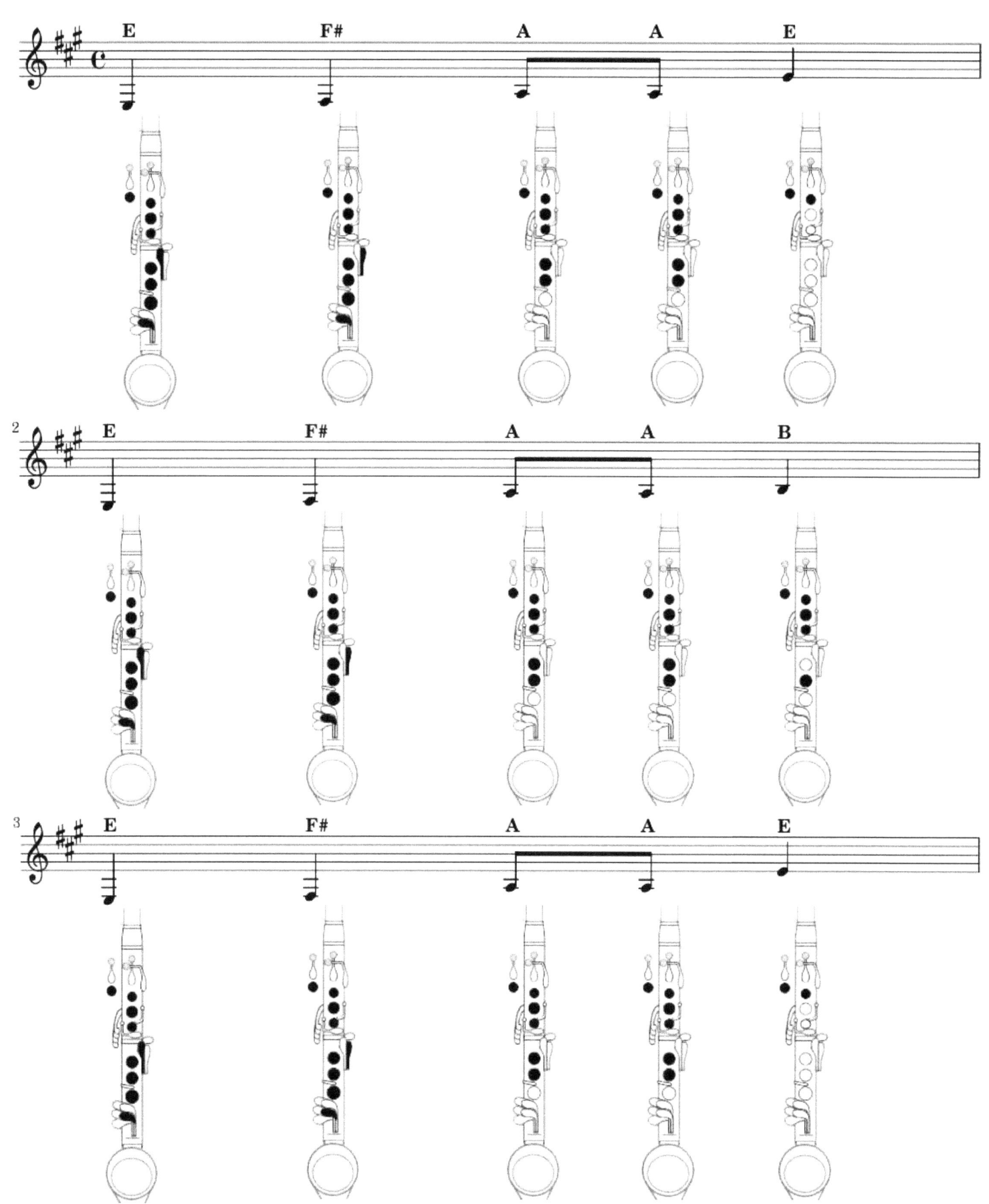

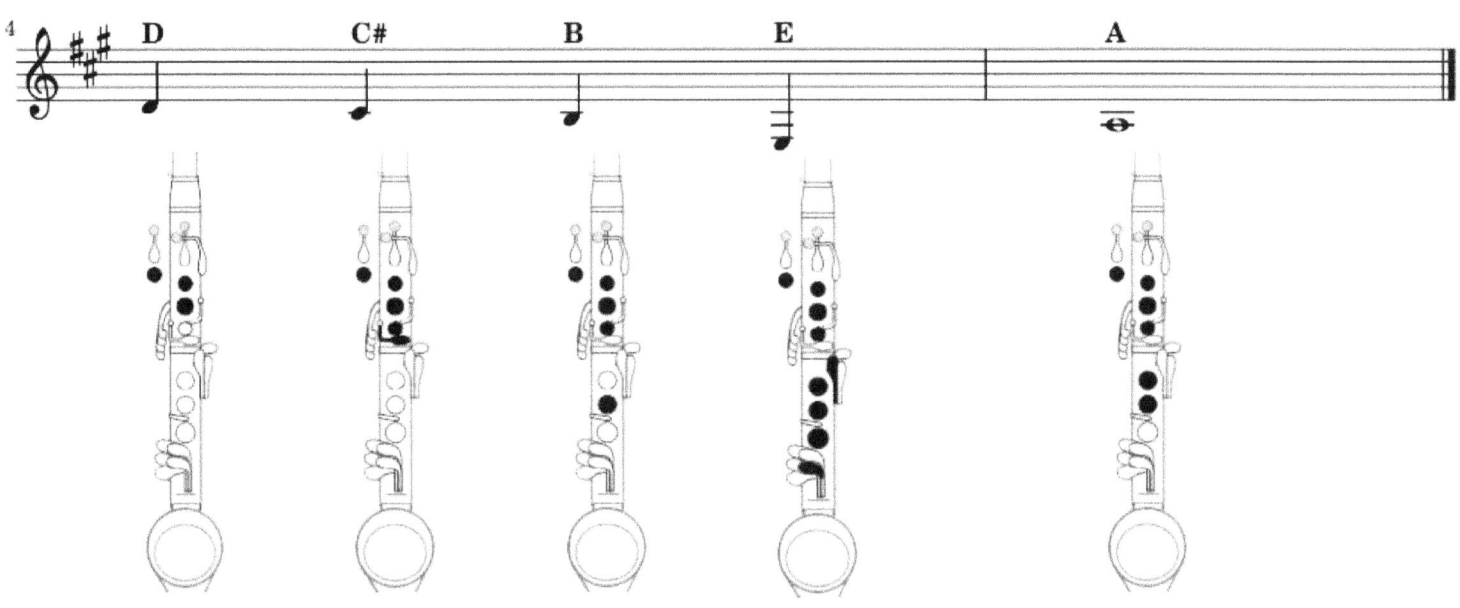

It's a Jazzy Day!

This one is a tune that hits the low notes and jumps an octave higher.

Scan the QR Code

to Listen to the song!

Tips for Playing Alto Clarinet

Learning to play the alto clarinet can be exciting, and like any new skill, it takes practice and patience. If you're just starting, these tips will help you get off to a great start. Remember, everyone was a beginner once, so don't feel discouraged if things don't sound perfect right away!

Tip #1: Press the Keys Properly
One of the most important parts of playing the clarinet is making sure you're pressing the keys properly. If your fingers don't press the keys enough to seal the holes completely, the sound will be squeaky or not come out at all. To fix this, check that your fingers are curved naturally and resting gently over the holes. You don't need to press super hard, just enough to create a good seal. Practicing in front of a mirror can help you see if your fingers are in the right place.

Tip #2: Keep Your Hands Relaxed
It's easy to tense up your hands when you're trying to play a tricky note or learn something new. However, tight hands can make it harder to move your fingers quickly and comfortably. Instead, try to relax your hands and use light pressure when pressing the keys. Think of it like typing on a keyboard, your fingers should move lightly and smoothly, not with a lot of force.

Tip #3: Take It Slow
When you're learning a new song or scale, it's tempting to play it fast to see how it sounds. But going too fast can lead to mistakes and bad habits. Start by practicing slowly and focusing on getting each note right. As you build muscle memory in your fingers, you'll be able to play faster without even thinking about it. It's like riding a bike. Once your body knows what to do, everything gets easier!

Fun Fact: Alto Clarinet Fingerings and Other Instruments
Did you know that learning the alto clarinet can help you play other woodwind instruments in the future? Many woodwinds, like the saxophone or oboe, share similar fingerings for their lowest notes. That means if you've mastered the basics on the alto clarinet, you're already one step closer to trying something new. Who knows? Maybe the clarinet is just the beginning of your musical journey!

Make Music!
Starting an instrument like the alto clarinet is an adventure. With a little practice and these tips in mind, you'll be playing your favorite tunes in no time. Remember to have fun, take breaks, and celebrate every small success. Before you know it, you'll be making beautiful music that you, and everyone around you, can enjoy!

Ring Around the Rosie

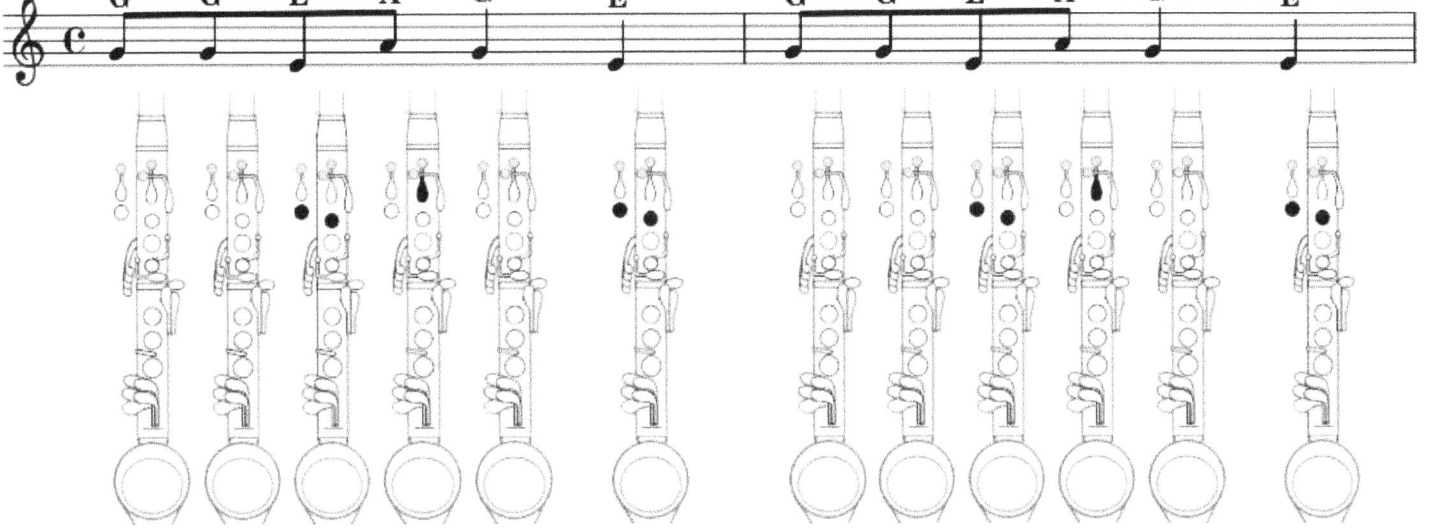

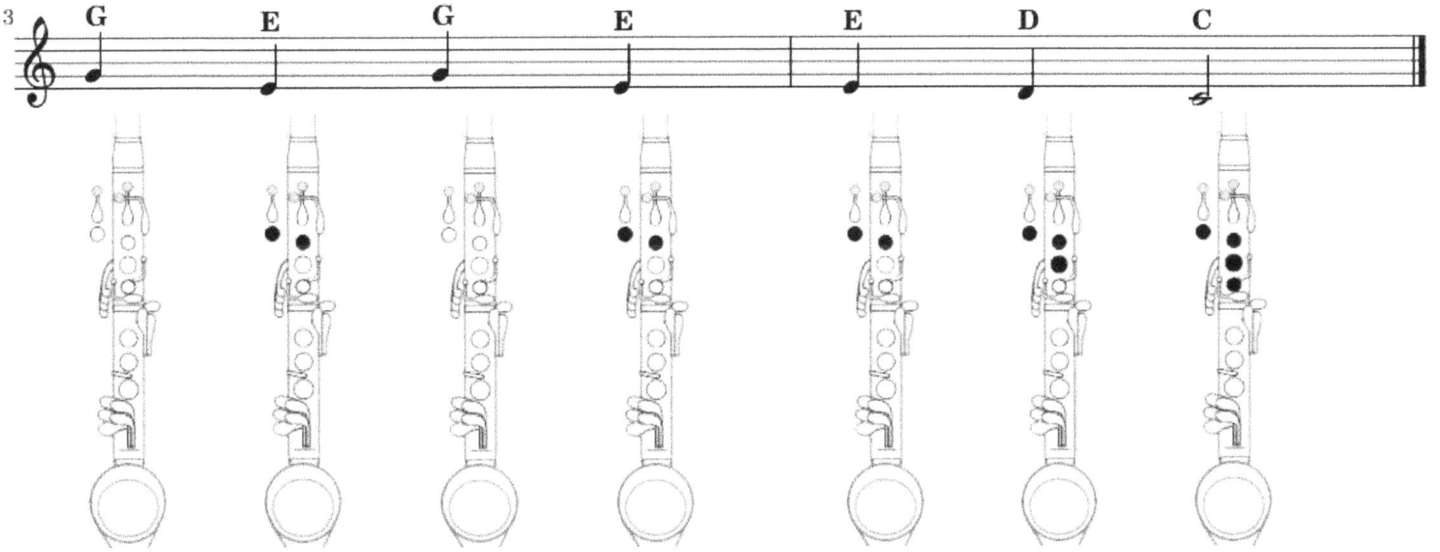

43

G G E A G E G G E A G E

G E G E E D C

Scan the QR Code

to Listen to the song!

Pop Goes the Weasel

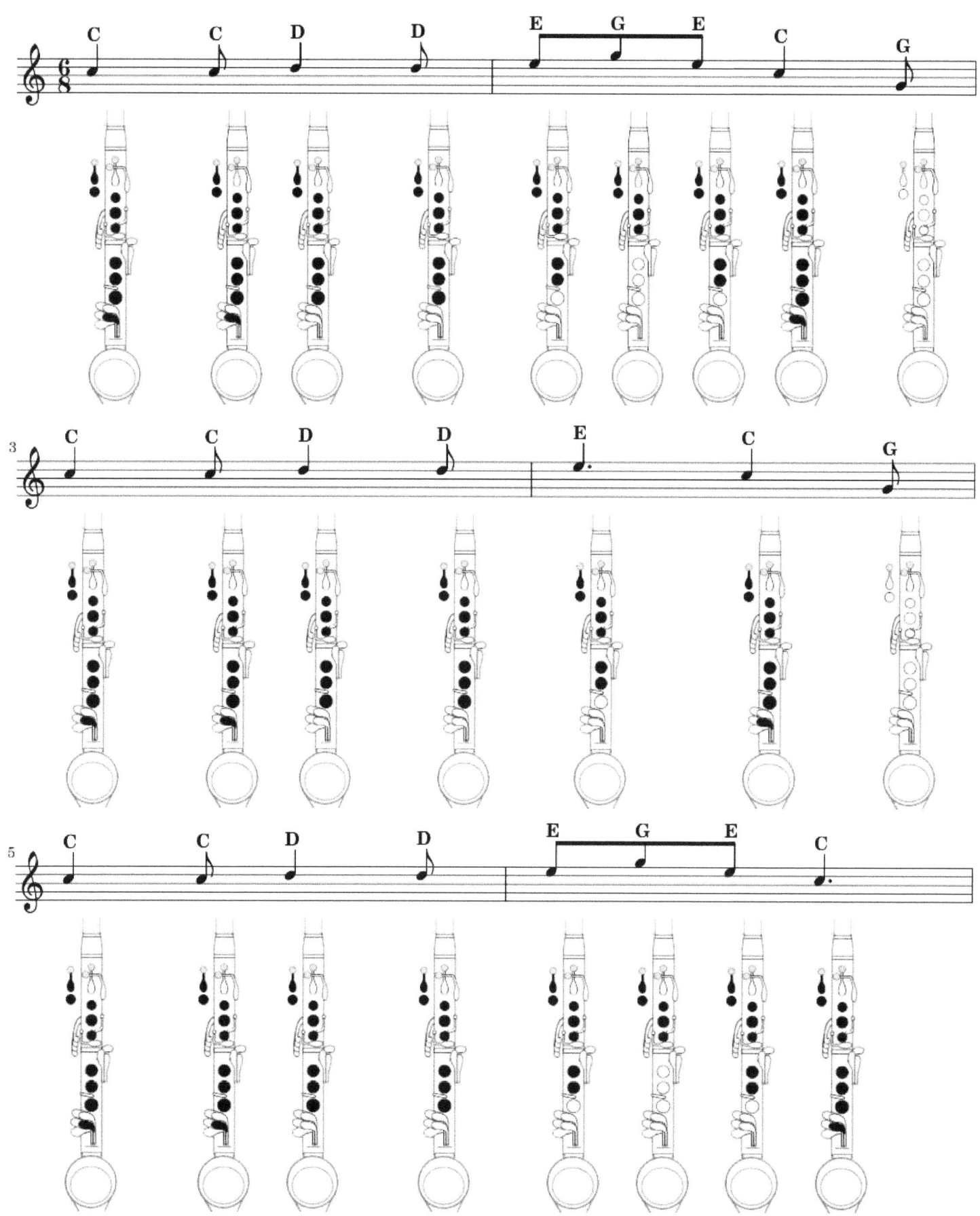

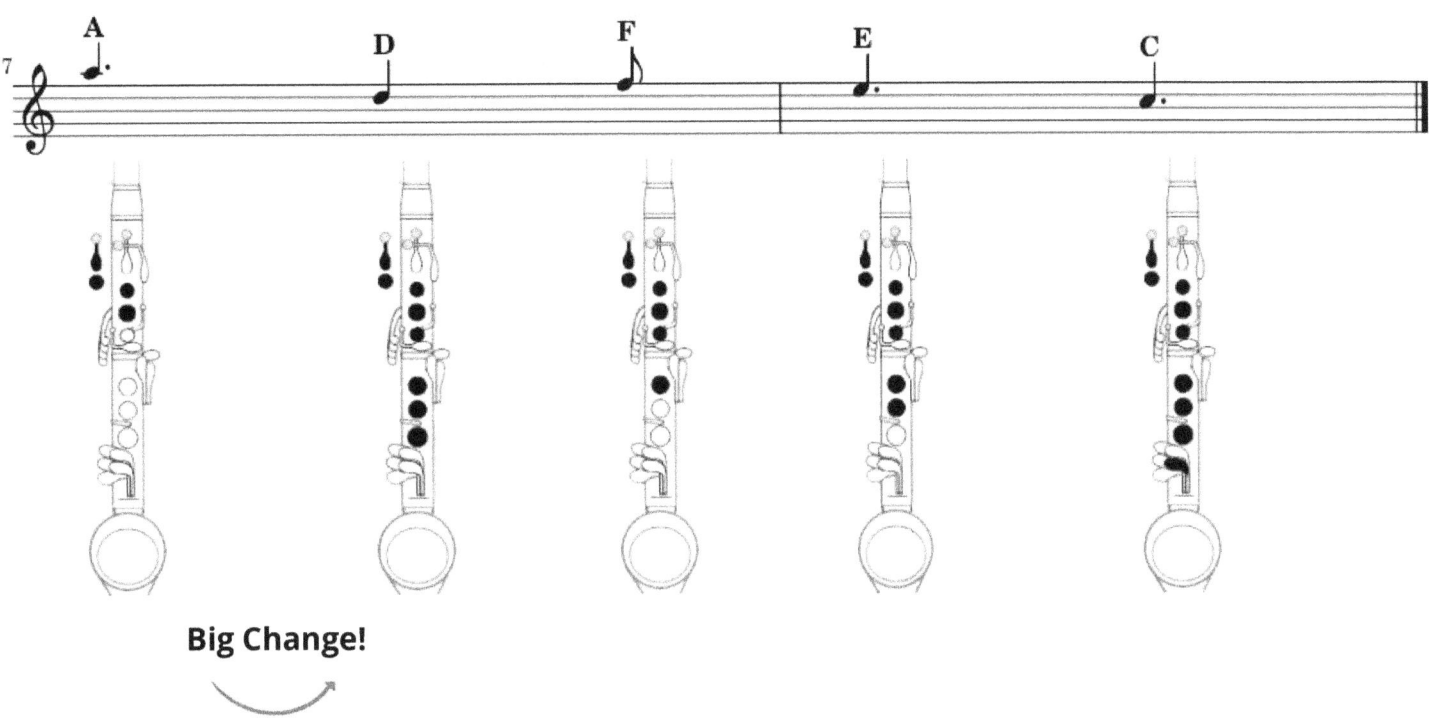

Big Change!

Going slowly, practice playing A to D to A to D to A seven times in a row. Keep your fingers close and your air steady. Soon you'll be able to make that big change without even thinking about it.

"Pop Goes the Weasel" is a fun and catchy tune that's been around since the 1850s. It first became popular in England, where people sang it in music halls and danced to it. No one knows for sure what the words mean, but one theory is that "pop" meant to pawn something, like selling your coat ("weasel" was a slang word for coat). The song talks about spending money and everyday life in London. Over time, the lyrics changed, and in the United States it became a children's rhyme about a monkey chasing a weasel around a mulberry bush. Even though the meaning is a bit of a mystery, the song has stayed popular for over 150 years because of its fun rhythm and surprising "pop!"

Scan the QR Code

to Listen to the song!

Camptown Races

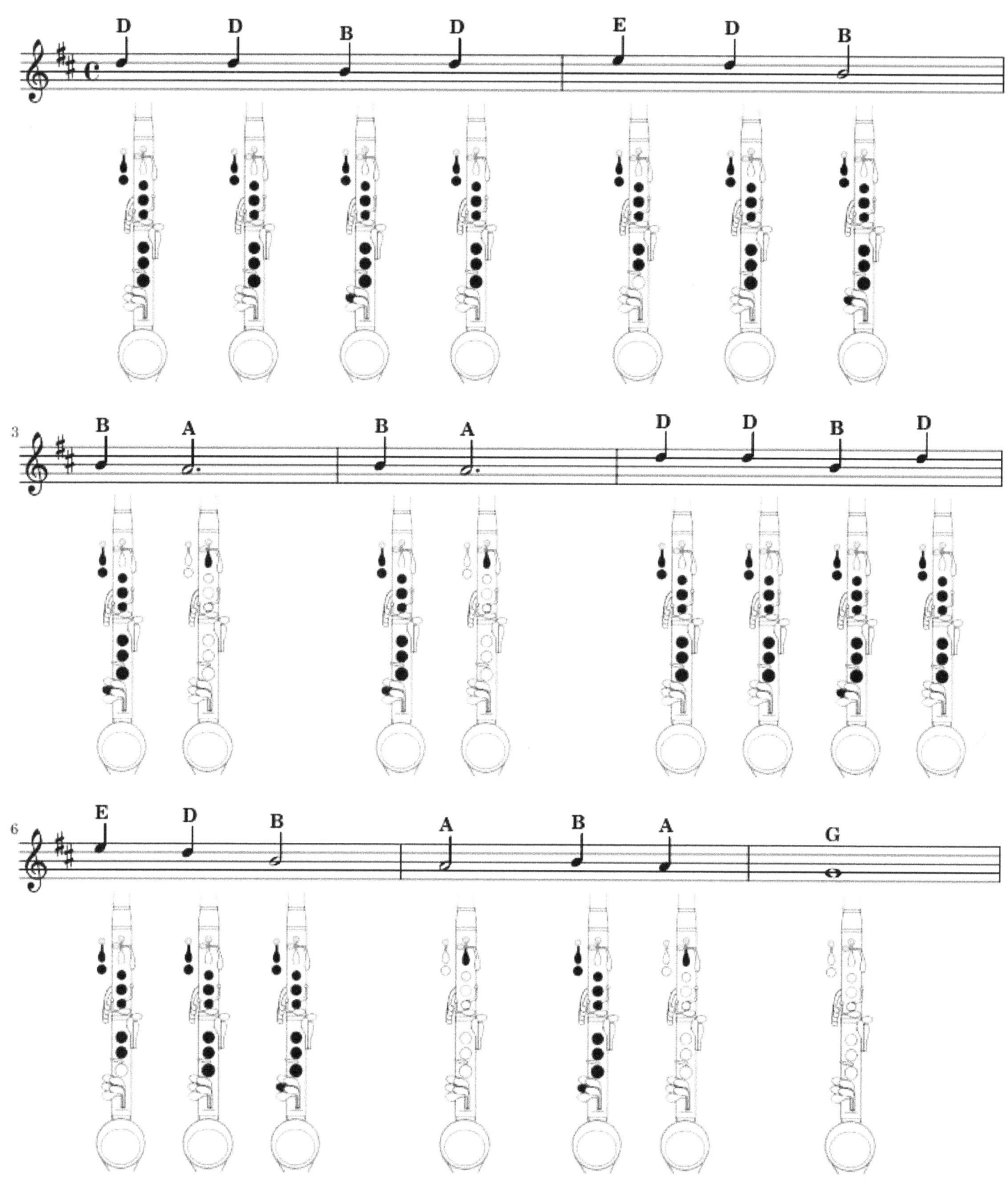

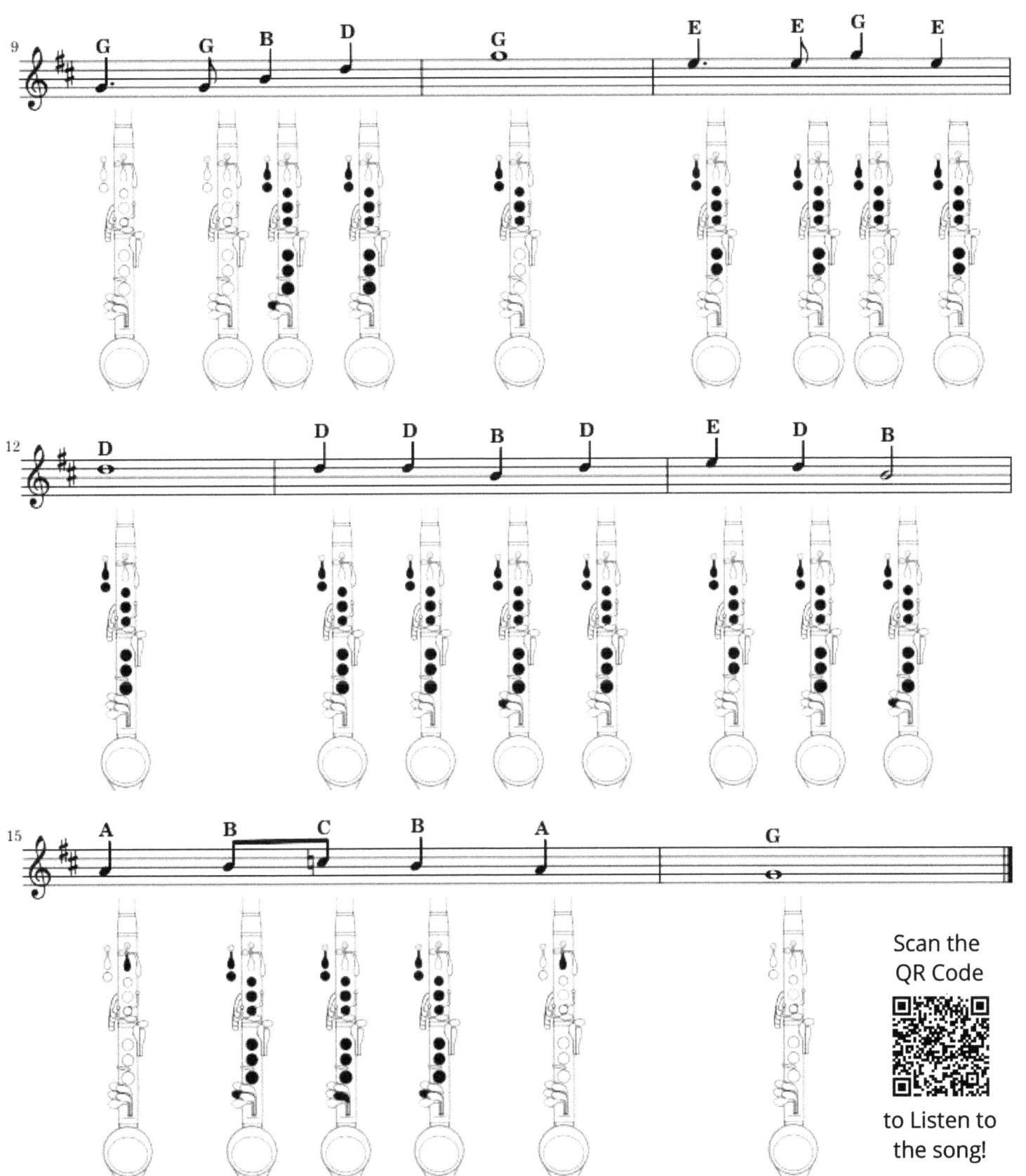

Row Row Row Your Boat

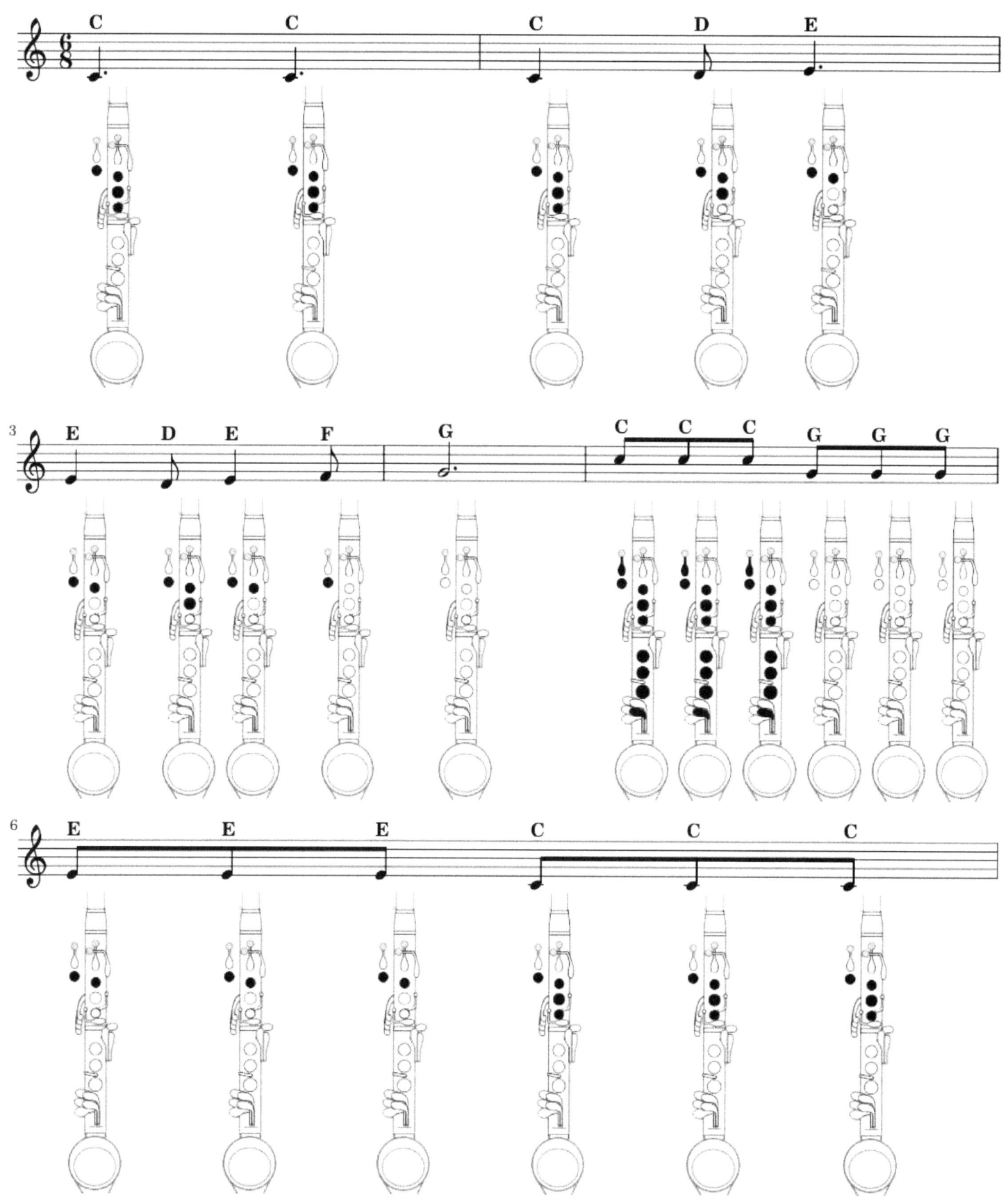

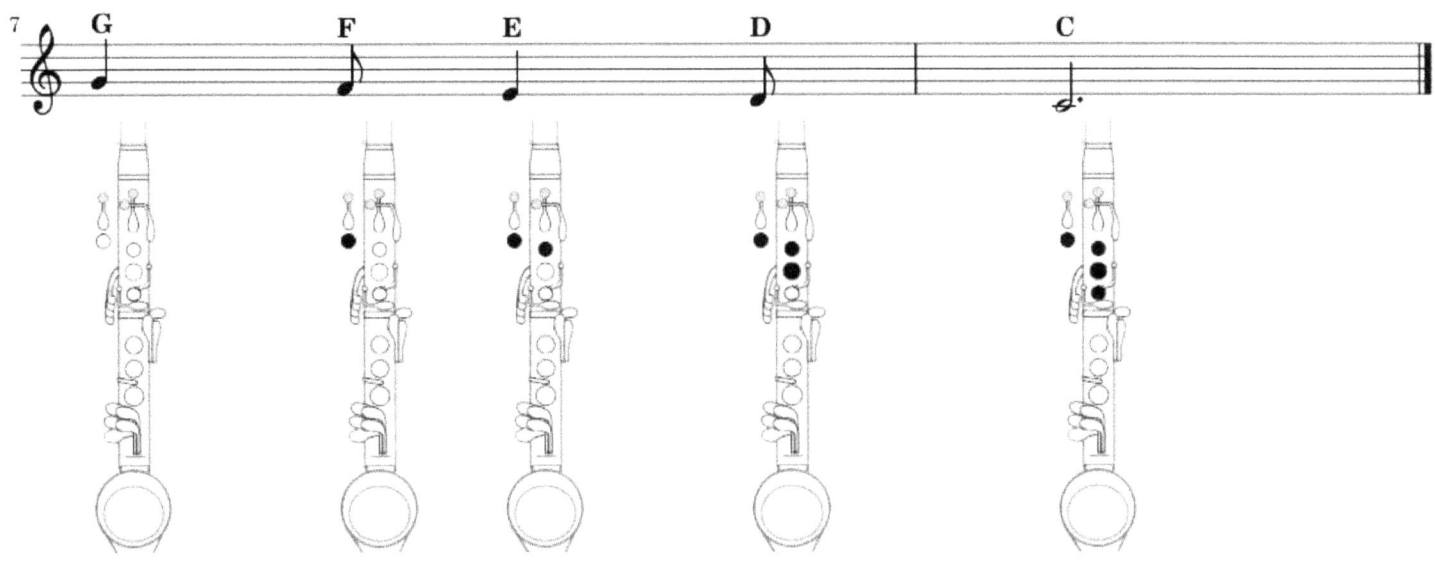

"Row, Row, Row Your Boat" is one of the most well-known children's songs in the English-speaking world. It first appeared in print in the 1850s, and its simple melody and lyrics have made it easy for people of all ages to sing and remember. The song is often sung as a round, where one group starts and another joins in a few beats later, creating a layered harmony. While it sounds playful, the words also carry a quiet message: life moves gently forward, like rowing a boat down a stream. It reminds us to stay calm, enjoy the ride, and not take things too seriously.

Scan the QR Code

to Listen to the song!

Hot Cross Buns

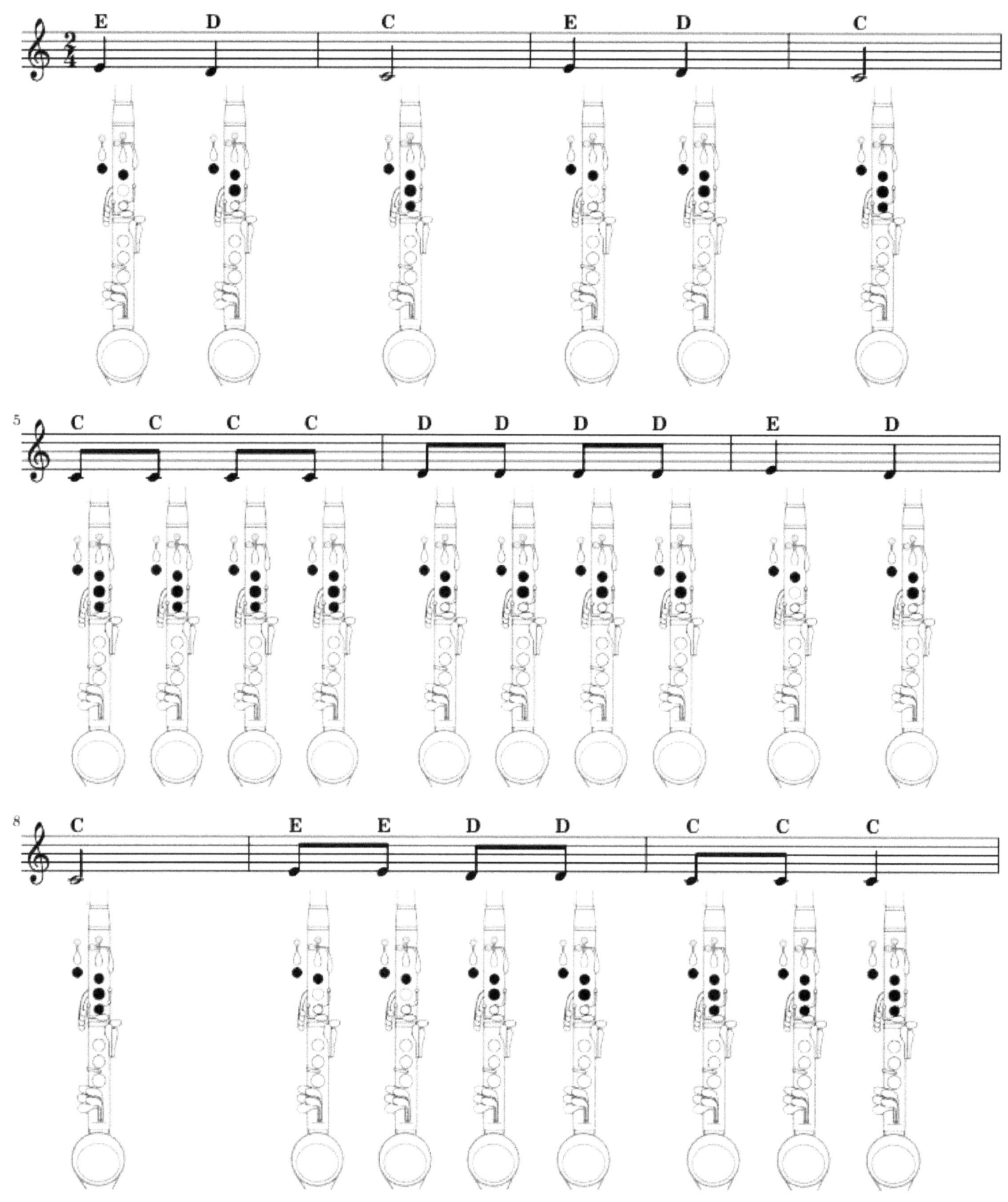

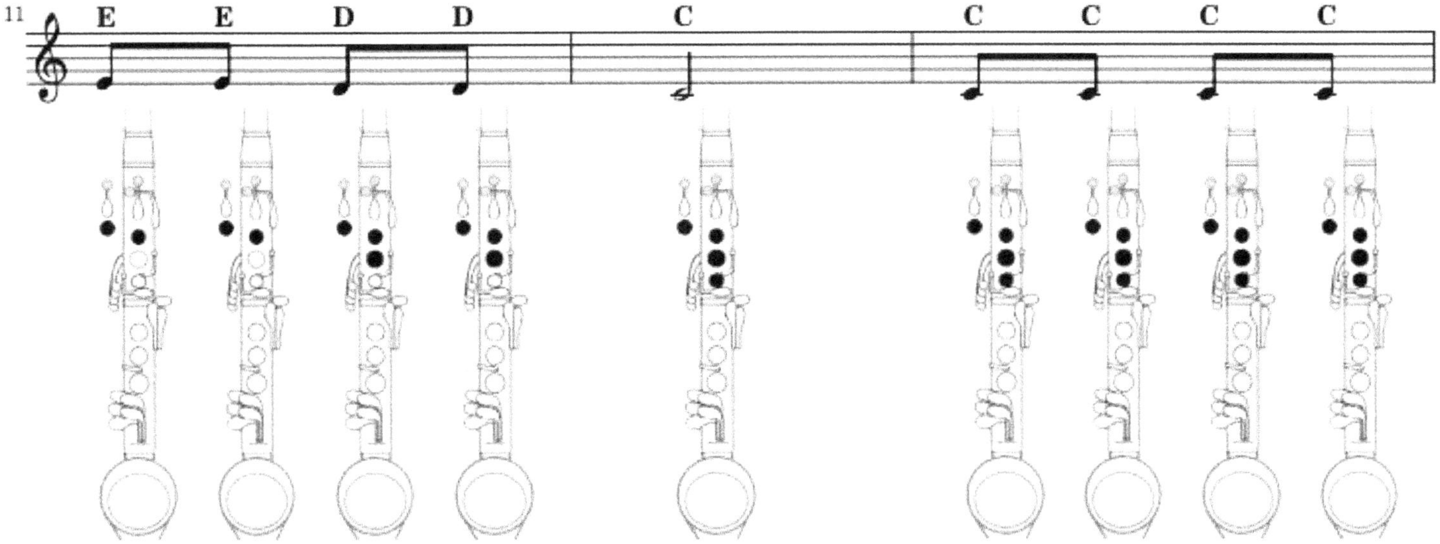

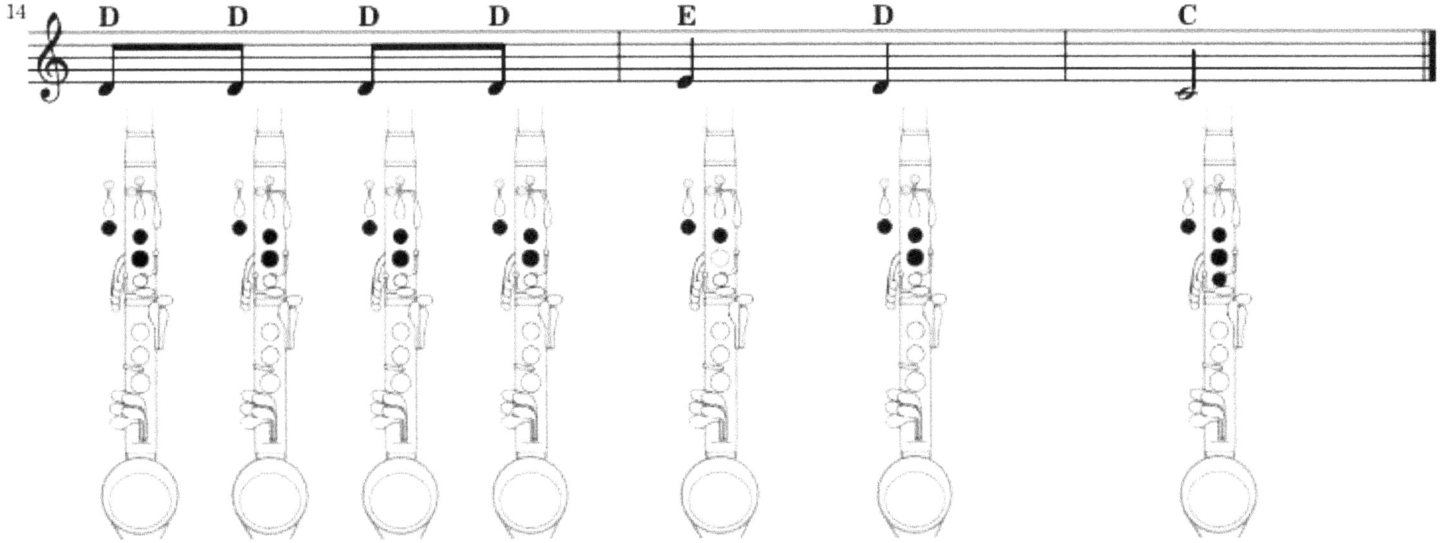

London Bridge is Falling Down

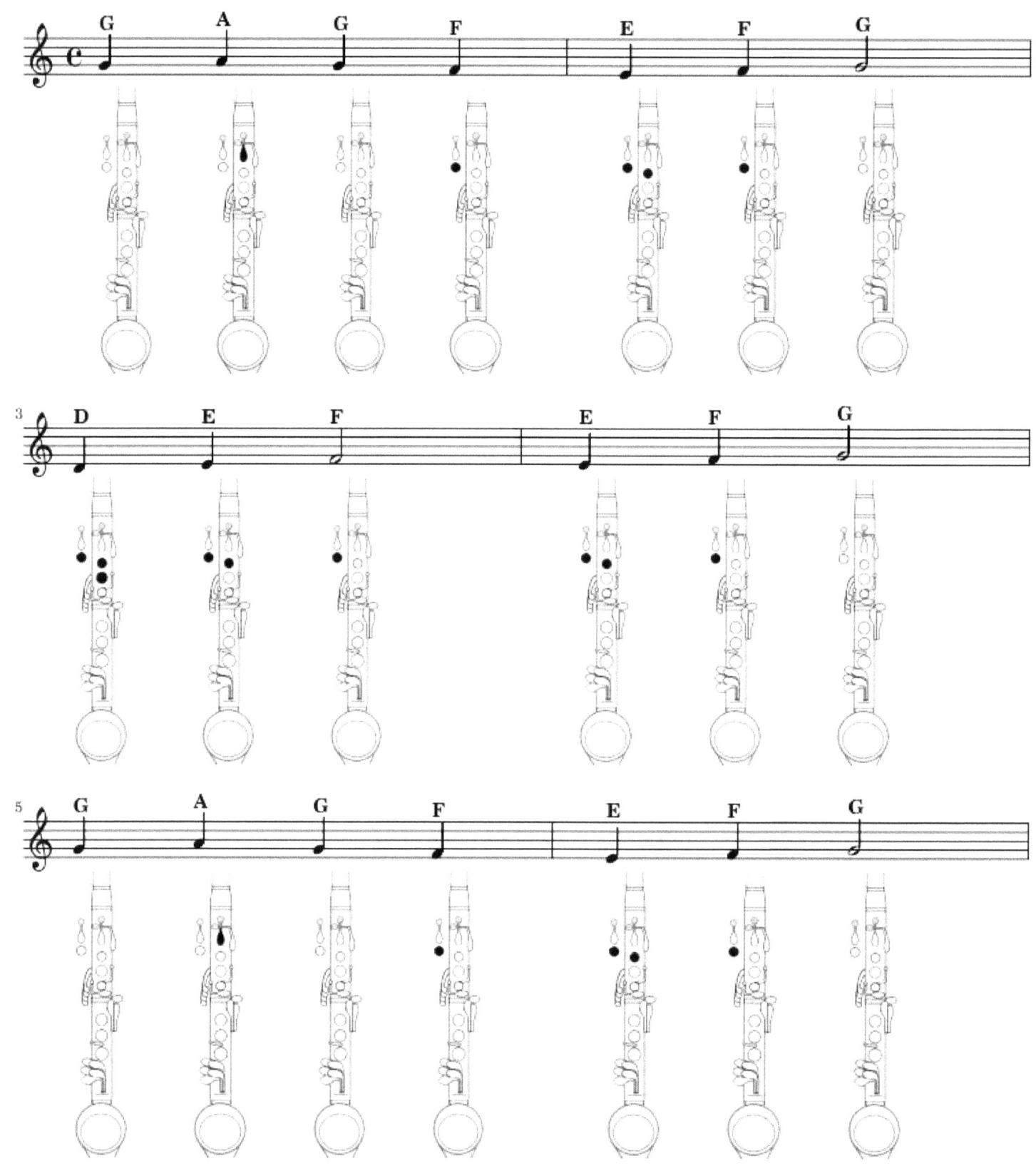

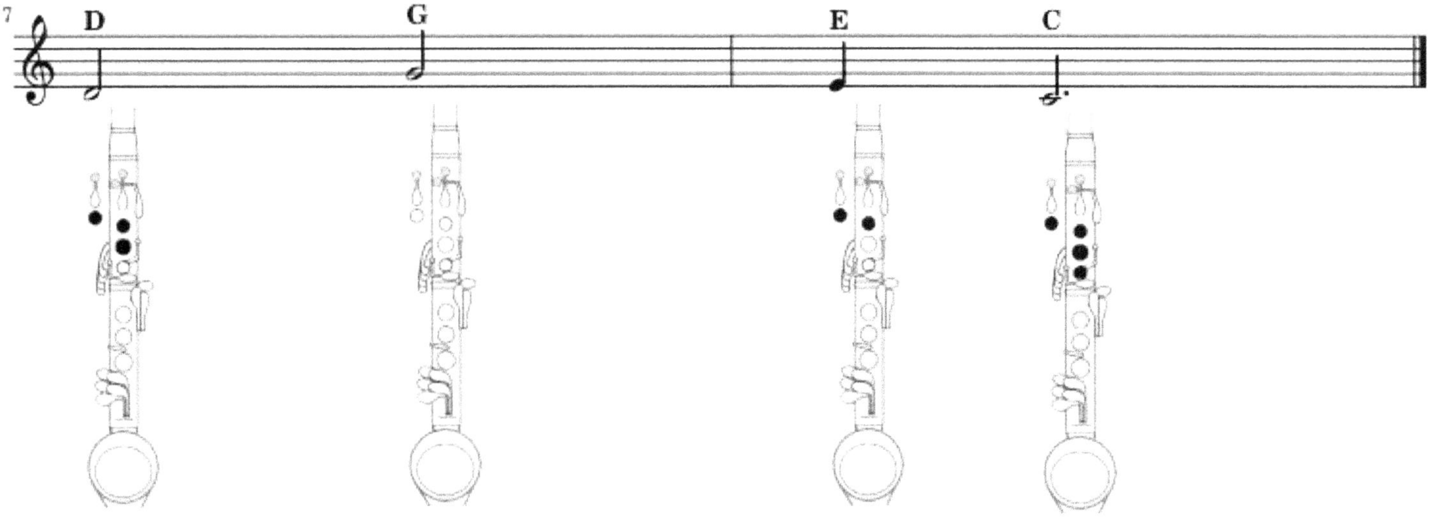

This song is about London Bridge, one of the oldest bridges across the River Thames in London, England. Over the centuries, this famous bridge was built, broken, rebuilt, and repaired many times. The earliest versions go back to the medieval era, when wooden bridges were often destroyed by fires, floods, or even invading armies.

Today, the modern London Bridge is made of concrete and steel, and it's not falling down anytime soon. But the song lives on, reminding us that even strong things can need help, and history can hide inside even the simplest games.

Scan the QR Code

to Listen to the song!

That's What's the Matter

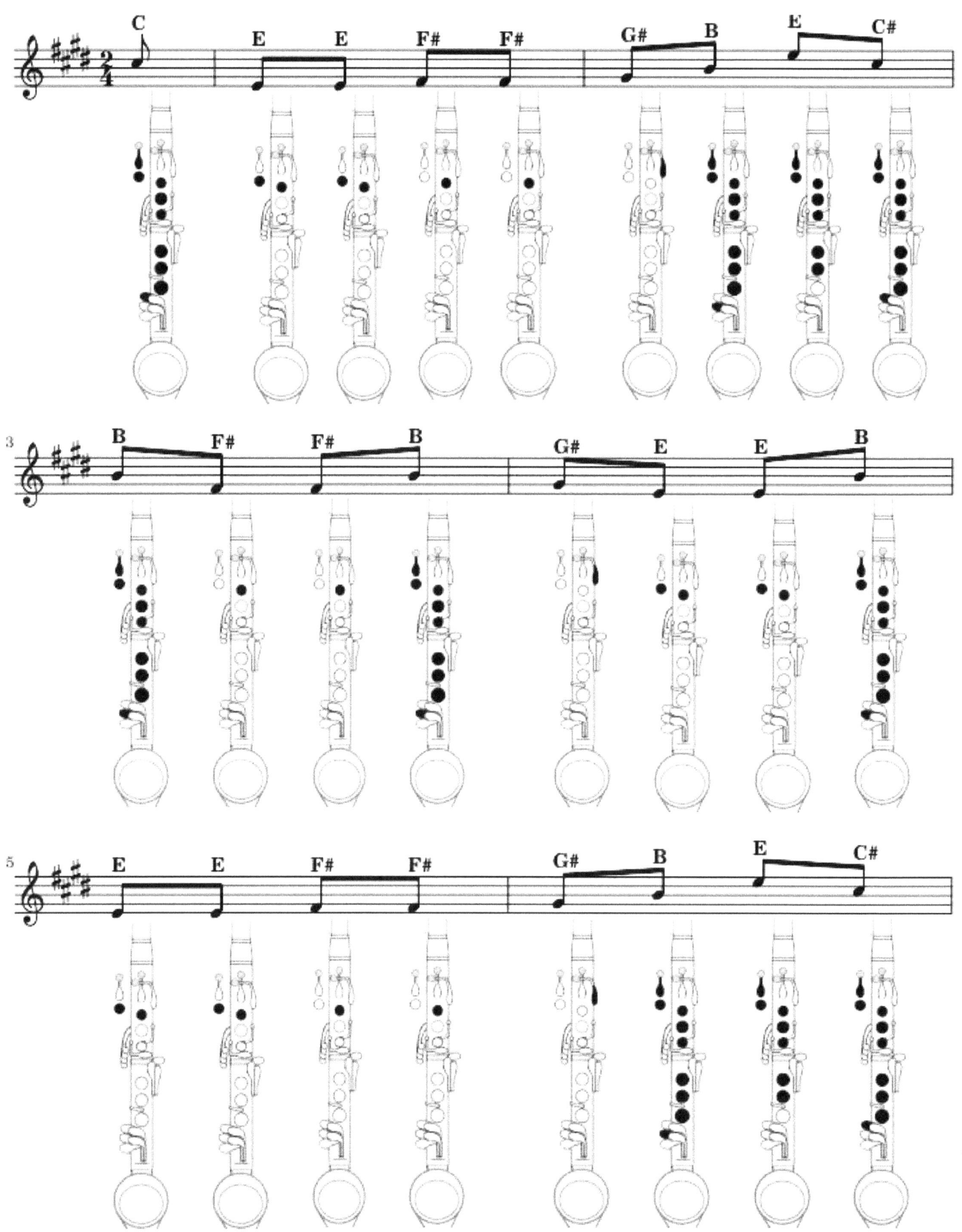

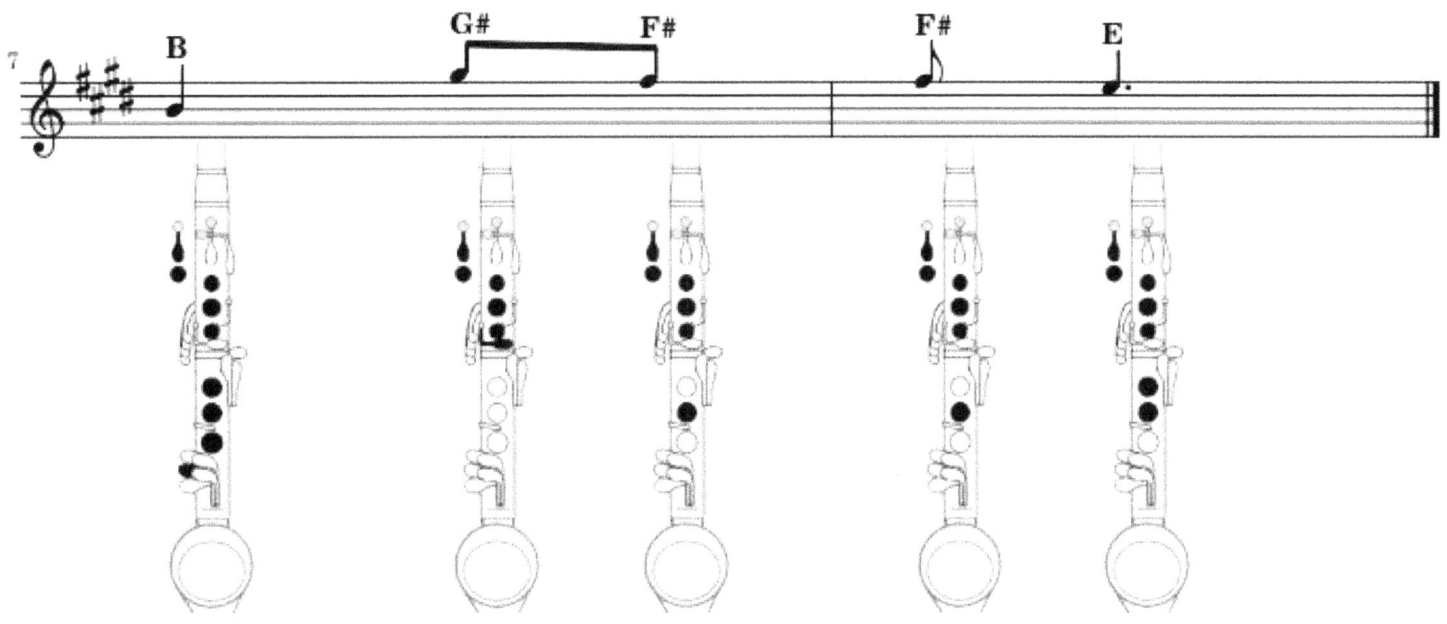

"That's What's the Matter" is a tune written by Stephen Foster in 1862. It was arranged for piano and played by instruments like clarinet, flute, or violin. The melody is upbeat and full of energy, showing the popular musical style of the 1800s. It's a fun piece to play and a great example of music people enjoyed at home and in small-town gatherings during that time.

Scan the QR Code

to Listen to the song!

She'll Be Comin' 'Round the Mountain

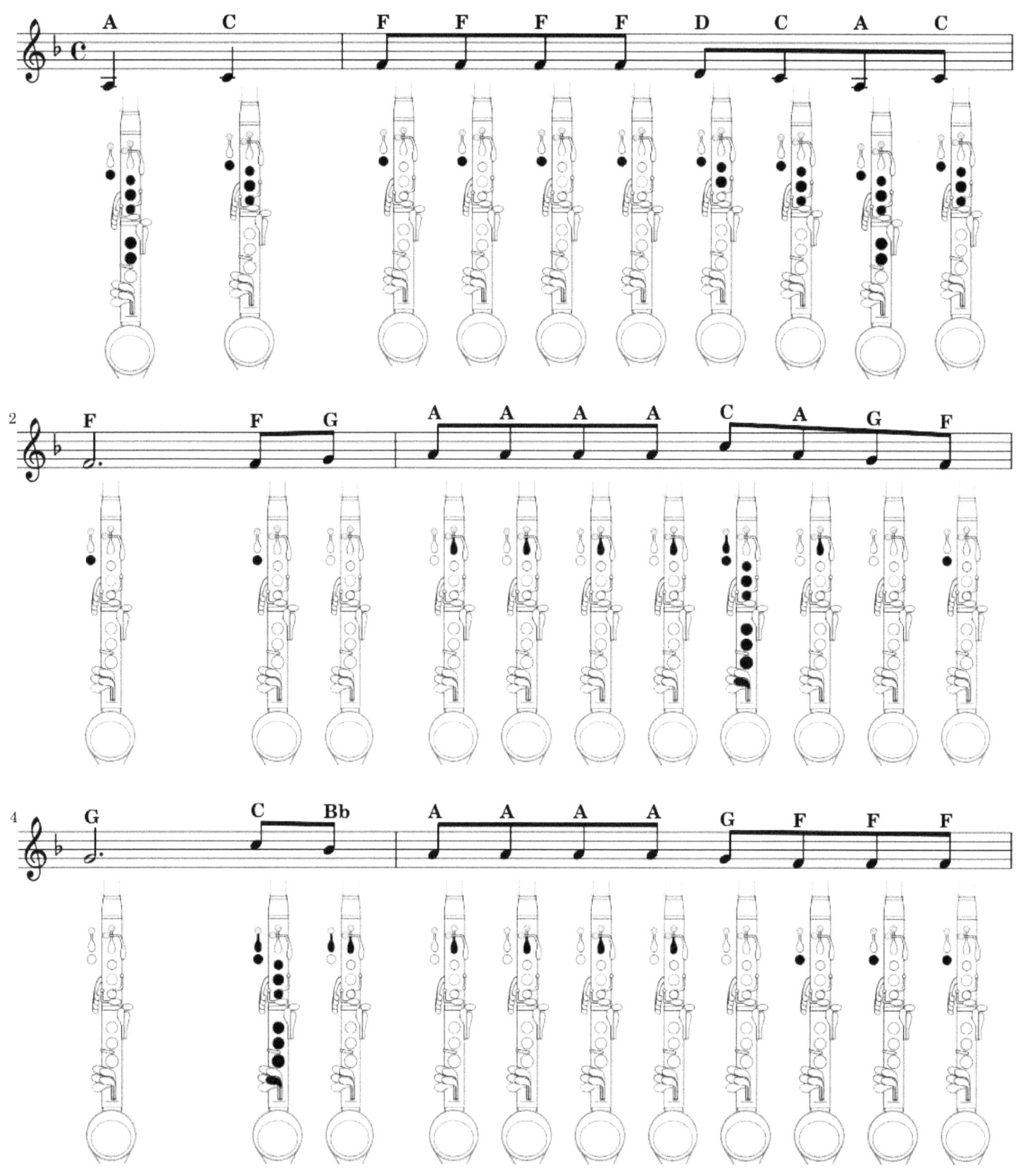

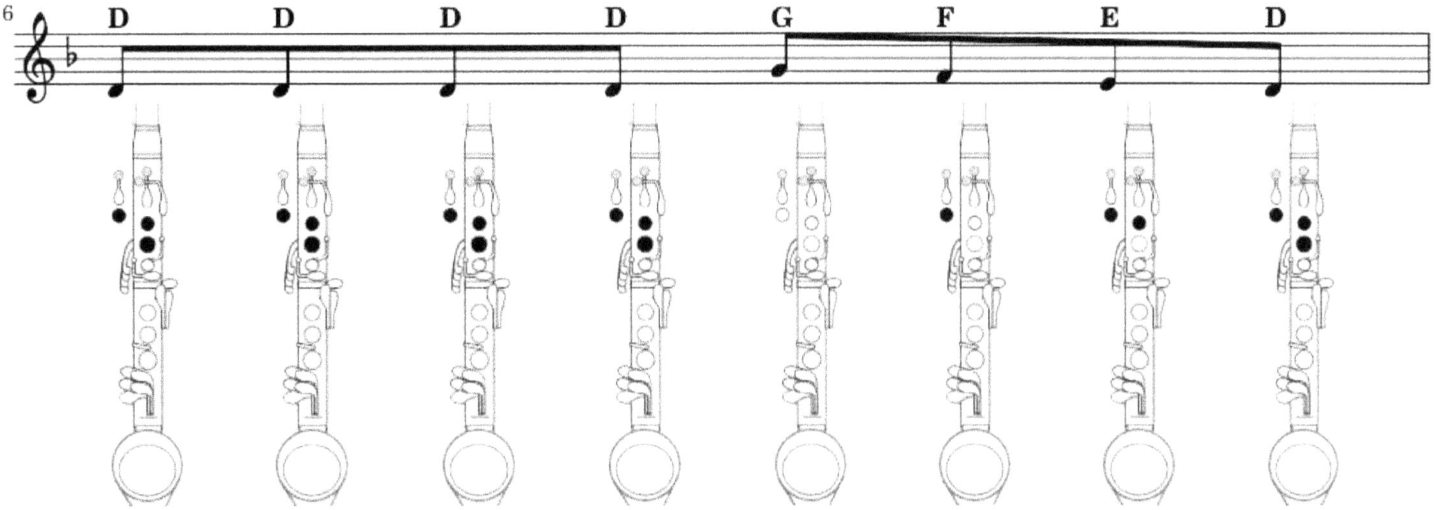

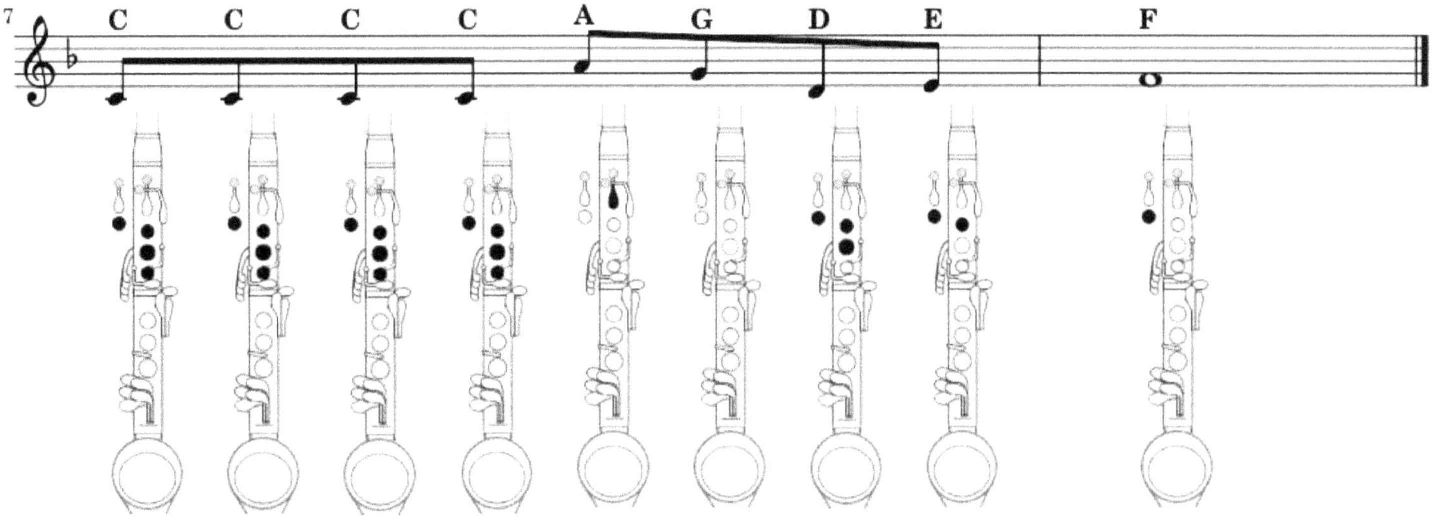

Jingle Bells

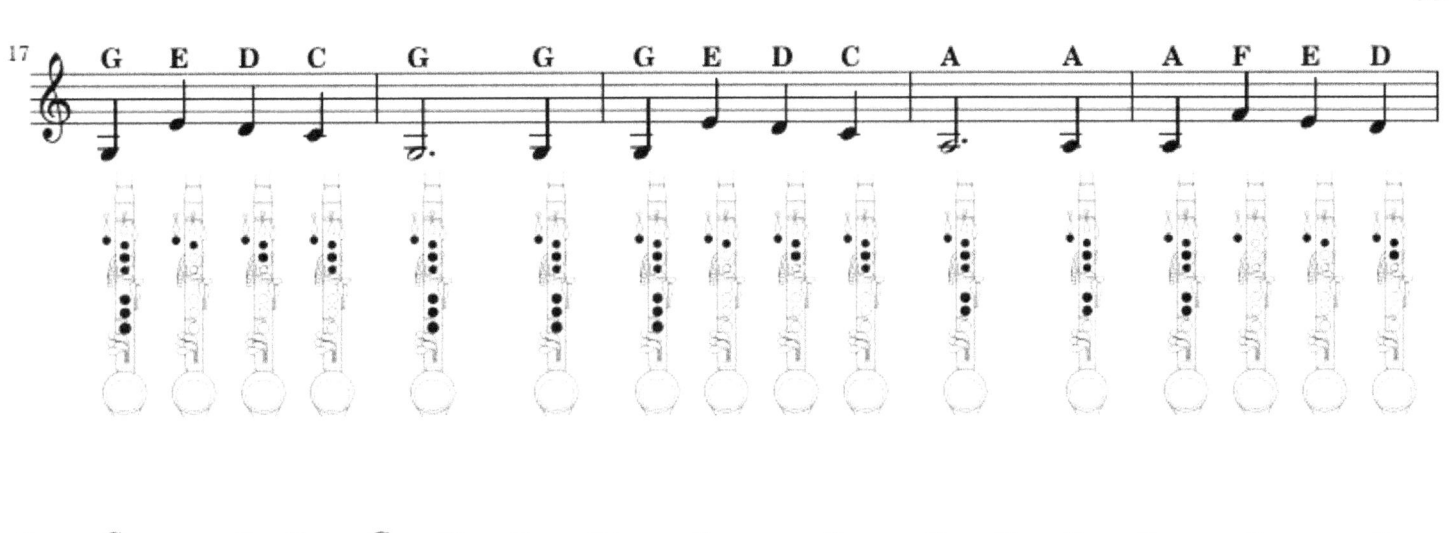
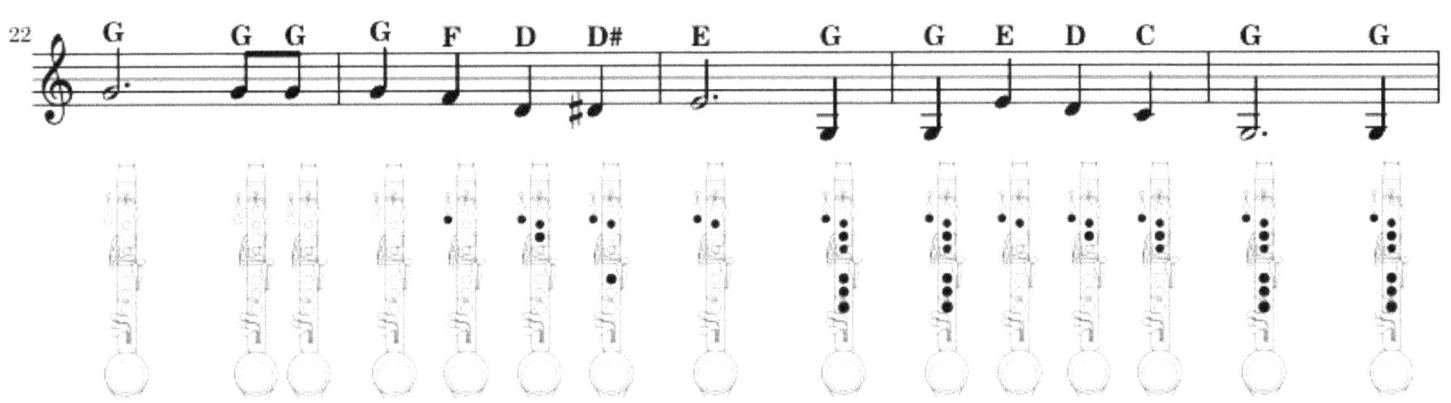

Scan the QR Code to Listen to the song!

This Old Man

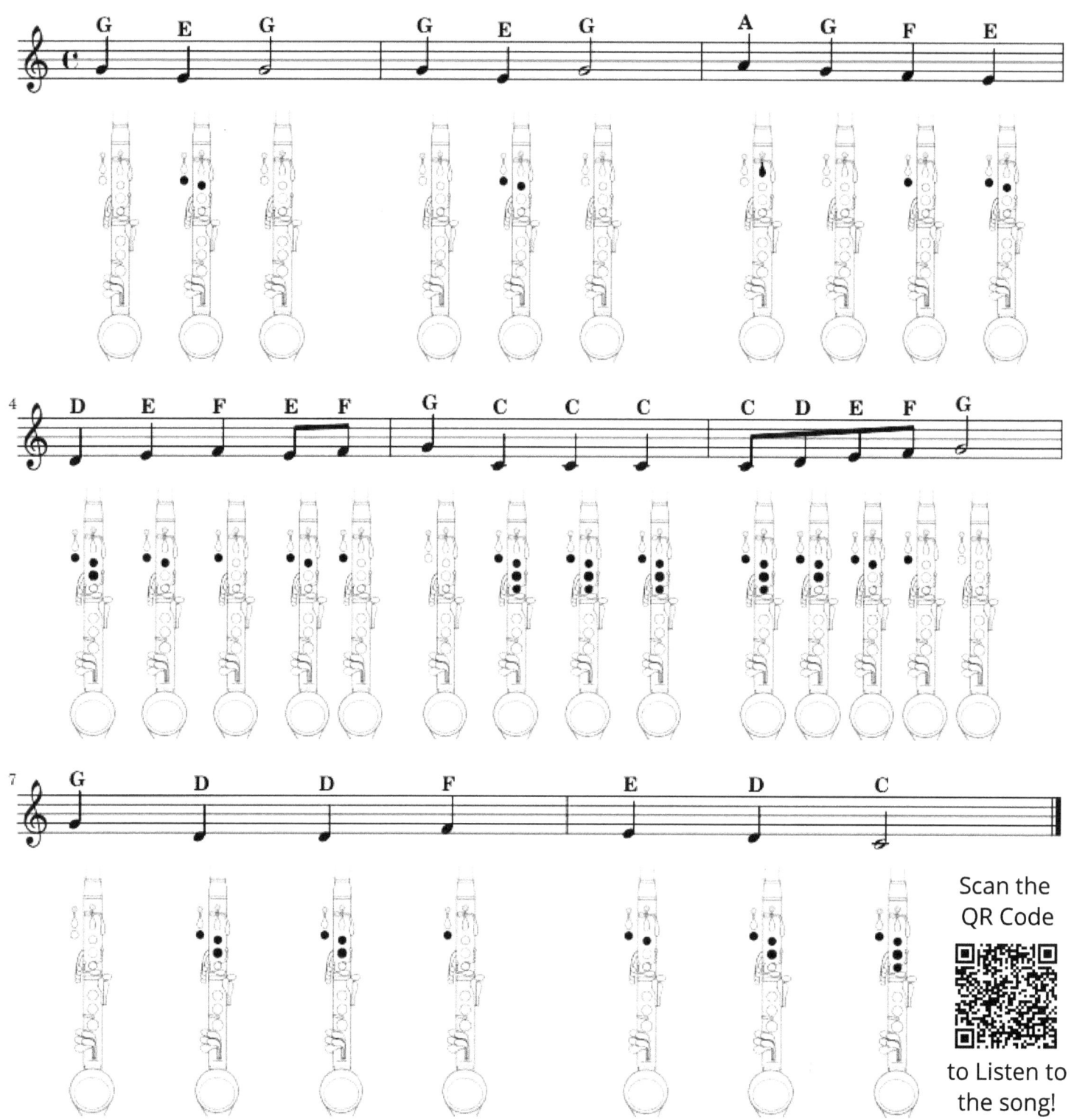

E♭ Alto Clarinet Fingering Chart

The E♭ Alto Clarinet fingering chart begins with the note E♭3 (E flat 3), the lowest note playable on the instrument. Next, the chart rises note by note, showing flats (♭) and sharps (#), all the way up to C6.

The numbers 3, 4, 5, and 6 are called octave numbers. Octave numbers are the numbers you see next to a note name, like E♭3 or C6. They tell you how high or low a note sounds on your instrument or in music. Each time you go from one C note to the next higher sounding C note, you move up one octave and the number goes up by one also. So, the number helps show which version of the note you're playing, low, middle, or high.

Some notes have more than one way to place your fingers. These other fingerings are shown as smaller alto clarinets aside the primary fingering used in this book. Try them!

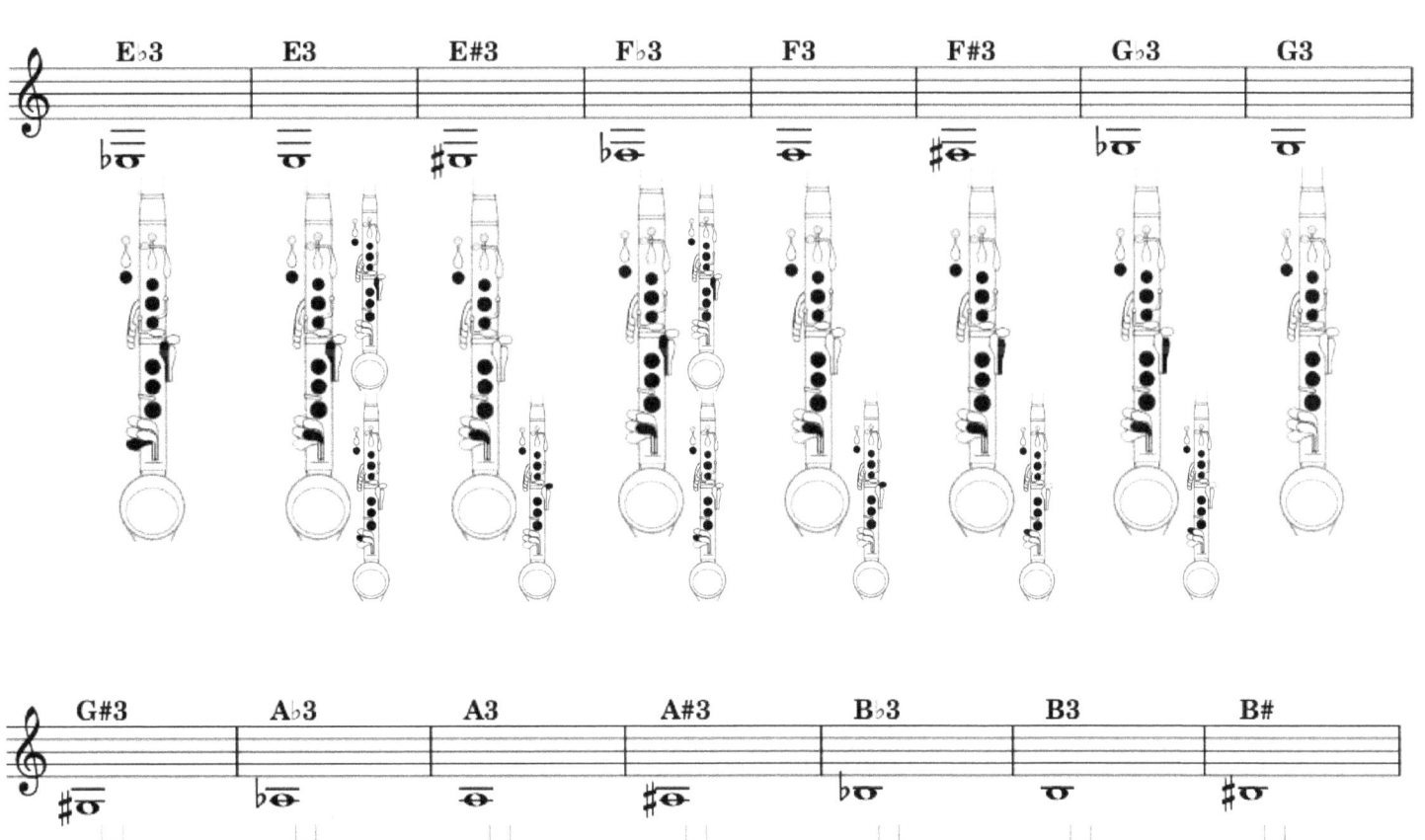

Some notes have more than one way to place your fingers. These other fingerings are shown as smaller alto clarinets aside the primary fingering used in this book. Try them!

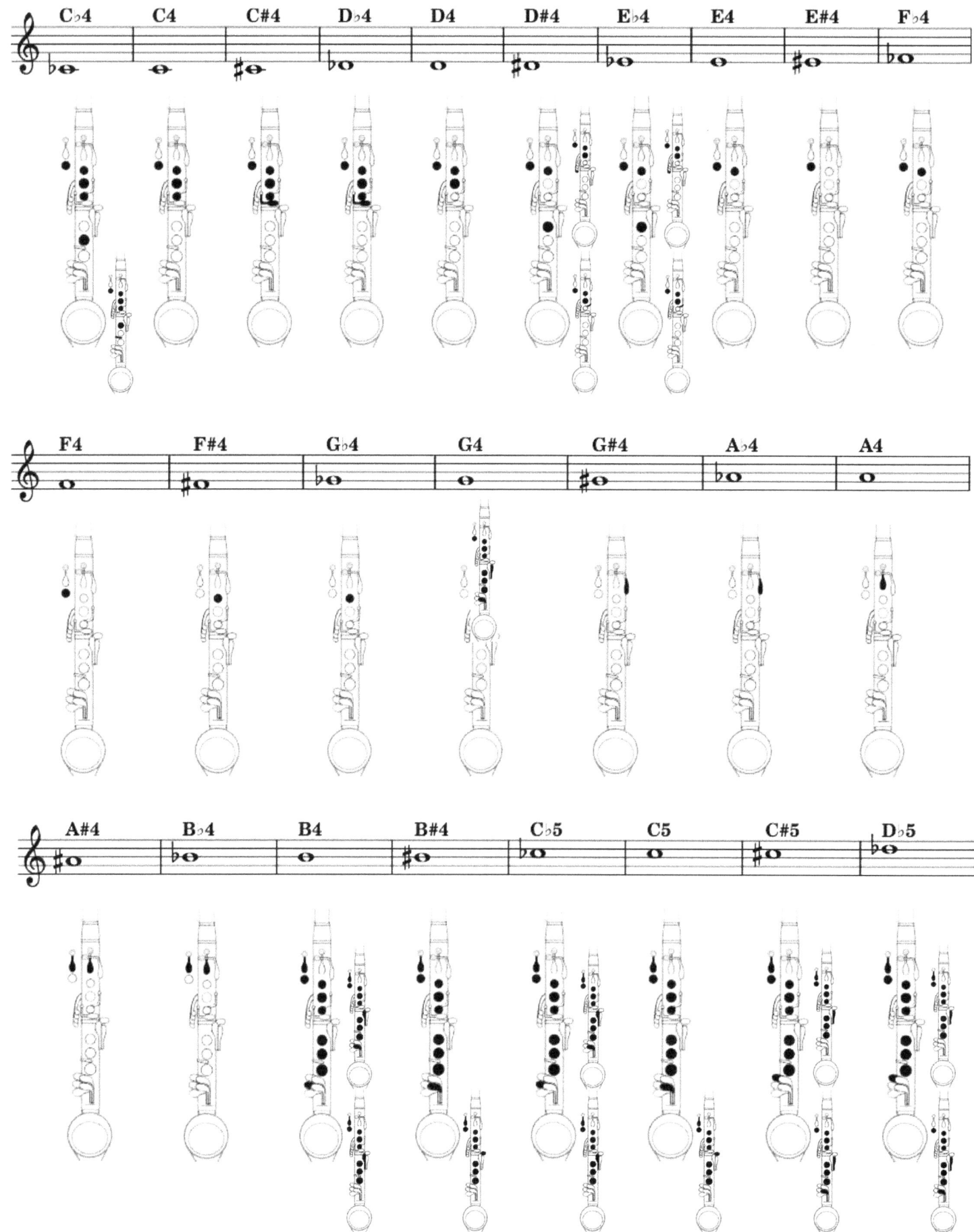

Some notes have more than one way to place your fingers. These other fingerings are shown as smaller alto clarinets aside the primary fingering used in this book. Try them!

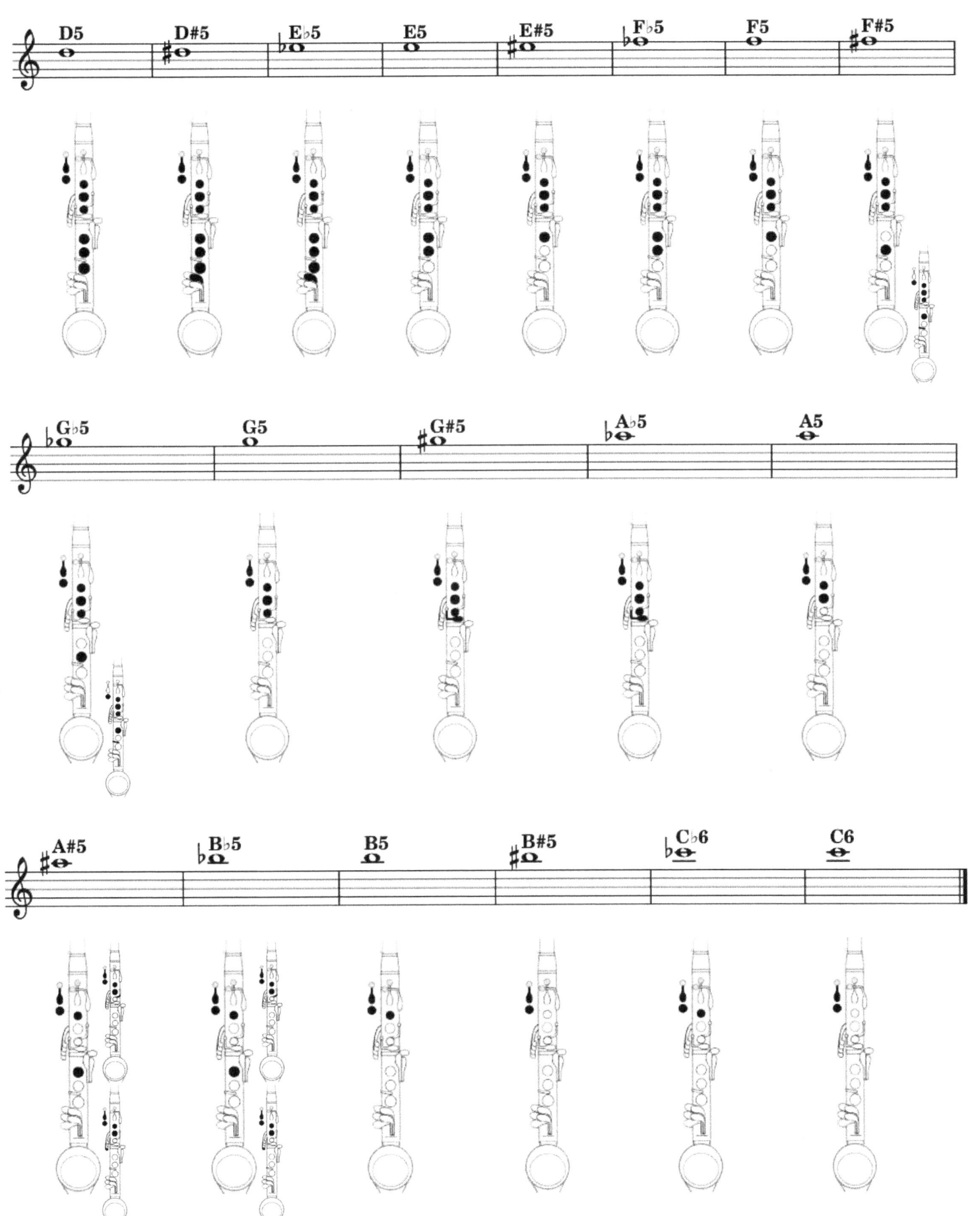

E♭ Alto Clarinet History

The E♭ alto clarinet was developed in the early 1800s during a period of intense innovation in woodwind instrument design. As musical ensembles grew in size and range, instrument makers began expanding the clarinet family to include higher and lower voices.

One of the earliest known alto clarinets was created by Iwan Müller, a German clarinetist and inventor, around 1808 to 1810. Müller had already made significant improvements to the soprano clarinet's key system and was experimenting with new forms that could fill the tonal space between the standard clarinet and the larger bass versions.

The modern E♭ alto clarinet, with its distinctive curved metal neck and bell, was refined and brought closer to its present form by Adolphe Sax in the 1840s. Best known as the inventor of the saxophone, Sax contributed to the evolution of several wind instruments intended for military bands, and his workshop produced early examples of alto clarinets with enhanced projection and tuning stability.

The instrument was designed to strengthen the middle voice of the clarinet section, supporting harmonies and bridging the gap between the higher and lower registers. It added warmth, depth, and flexibility to concert and military bands, which were becoming more complex in their arrangements.

By the early 20th century, the E♭ alto clarinet had secured a place in American school bands and wind ensembles, where it was commonly written into band literature. The instrument still holds its place in clarinet choirs and contemporary compositions, offering a distinct tonal color and a vital midrange voice in larger clarinet sections.

E♭ Alto Clarinet

www.ingramcontent.com/pod-product-compliance
Lightning Source LLC
LaVergne TN
LVHW061316060426
835507LV00019B/2179